M000237397

Discovering Hope in the Psalms is a delightful, life-changing book. These are hard tin
just finished 22 months of battling 4 different cancers. I know what it means to need hope. And I know of no better place to go
for hope than the Psalms. The authors provide a careful, practical treatment of selected psalms that offer hope. I highly recommend this book and am thankful to God for its release.

JP Moreland, Ph.D., Biola University distinguished professor, coauthor of *The Lost Virtue of Happiness*

As a women's ministry leader, pastor's wife, and author, I've done countless Bible studies, most written by big name authors. This study on Psalms by Pam Farrel, Jean E. Jones, and Karla Dornacher is one of the best. Jean has a way of taking biblical knowledge and leading readers into personal depth. Filled with insight, this study will leave you a deeper worshiper, more in love with God. For any believer who longs for more, this study is for you.

Donna Jones, speaker and author of *Seek*

Discovering Hope in the Psalms is a wonderful guide for learning to understand and live the rich truths of Psalms. Jones not only unpacks the historical and theological meaning of the Psalms, but provides practical exercises to personally experience these truths in your daily life. The chapters are short and easy to digest, and yet filled with meaning and depth. As this book helps you to worship God through the Psalms, you will be encouraged and blessed.

Sean McDowell, Ph.D., Biola University professor and author of *A New Kind of Apologist*

This book is like a gift filled with hope. It's one of the prettiest, more creative Bible studies I've found. Love it!

Linda Evans Shepherd, author of *Winning Your Daily Spiritual Battles*

This study is filled with hope, encouragement, and joyful expectation. The authors bring the text alive and ask the right questions to drive the message of the psalmist deep inside—where the Word of God can do its transformative work. This is a "must do" series for those who want to let a lot of light into the room during these darkening times.

Craig J. Hazen, Ph.D., Biola University apologetics program director and author of *Five Sacred Crossings*

Discovering Hope in the Psalms is a fresh new way to dive into Scripture. Each page is an invitation to embrace real hope found only in God's Word, while also providing fun ways to express truth with creativity.

Denise J. Hughes, author of the *Word Writers* Bible study series

A beautiful book that will fill your mind with solid teaching, stimulate your heart to creative expression, and lighten your soul with hope.

Janet Holm McHenry, speaker and author of *PrayerWalk*

What a rich treasury of insights, instruction, and inspiration. I can see this book being used over and over again, drawing the student into God's eternal truths resulting in a deeper level of hope.

Kathy Collard Miller, speaker and author of *Pure Hearted*

Never before have I seen a Bible study quite like this one! It invites readers to engage with their Creator with Bible wide open and colored pencils splayed all around! It is perfect for the seasoned Christian as well as those new to the faith, whether an "artist" or simply a woman who likes to doodle in the margins. All are welcome in the pages of this book, and will find great hope as they interact with God's living Word.

Wendy Speake, coauthor of *Life Creative*

I am thrilled with *Discovering Hope in the Psalms* because of its multifaceted approach to studying hope in the Bible. Not only do we dig into God's Word, but we learn how to practice it daily. We even have beautiful coloring pages to embrace all our senses. A must-read for anyone wanting to grow deeper with God.

Lucinda Secrest McDowell, author of *Dwelling Places*

Discovering Hope in the Psalms is a gift to all who open its pages. These women have produced a masterpiece!

Grace Fox, author of *Moving From Fear to Freedom*

Awaken the inner artist and allow hope in the Creator to fill your empty spaces and weary places.

Sharon Jaynes, author of *The Power of a Woman's Words*

For years, every morning I've found peace, inspiration, and solace in the Psalms. This book takes my experience to a new level—hope. Beyond the beauty of the words into the deep meaning and benefit of the verses.

Karen Porter, author of *Speak Like Jesus*

The Bible study is spiritually deep and theologically sound. It will encourage the reader to find hope in God through the Psalms, a hope we all need.

Clay Jones, D.Min., a Biola University professor and Ratio Christi chairman of the board

I believe women are going to get the maximum benefit from *Discovering Hope in the Psalms* because of the study's interactive nature and the opportunity to color and draw as we study God's Word.

Carole Lewis, author of *Live Life Right Here Right Now*

The authors and artist have created a fully immersive experience that draws participants into the Psalms and the refreshment of their hope-giving lessons. Every exquisite detail points to the Author and Artisan of hope.

Cynthia Ruchti, author of *A Fragile Hope*

Discovering Hope in the Psalms delivers an excitingly fresh Bible study *and* invites us into a Bible "QUEST." This book swells our hearts, delights our creativity, and engages our spirit for a full-on adventure of faith though timeless treasures of hope, restoration, and peace found only in God's Word. I passionately recommend this study!

Pat Layton, author of *Life Unstuck*

You will discover hope as you are drawn to the beauty of this study. Thank you, ladies, for illuminating the truth of the Word and doing it in such a creative way.

Kendra Smiley, author of *Mother of the Year*

The format of this study hooked me from day one! I felt like I was devoting and going deep with God as well as seeing things for the first time thanks to the helps and insights offered by Pam, Jean, and Karla. It is a treasure chest of connection with God on multiple levels.

Kenny Luck, president of Every Man Ministries and author of *Sleeping Giant*

A Bible study that is innovative, creative, and bursting with hope! As you intentionally dig deeper into the Psalms, creatively process what you discover, and prayerfully consider how to apply the truths taught, your life will change.

Becky Harling, author of *How to Listen So People Will Talk*

The creative team hit Refresh on the Psalms with this remarkable gem. The majesty and history of the psalms shine with new clarity and application with tools for every learning style.

Jane Rubietta, author of *Worry Less So You Can Live More*

This study makes the Bible applicable to real life and easy to understand. In a world that is drowning in watered-down Bible studies, *Discovering Hope in the Psalms* is a welcome and refreshing resource. I highly recommend it.

Shannon Kubiak Primicerio, author of *The Divine Dance*

This study is rich, rich, rich with hope-giving encouragement and inspiration. The authors have really nailed it with this one. Stunningly beautiful, with all kinds of creative responses and applications included, so that any woman can find an opportunity for a heart full of heaven-sent hope. Love this book!

Rhonda Rhea, TV personality and author of *Fix-Her-Upper*

As a women's ministry director, I am always in search of a Bible study that will truly make a difference in women's everyday lives. This study does just that, as the authors lead you in an experiential approach to *Discovering Hope in the Psalms*. You will not just learn about the God of hope, but your heart will be changed. I highly recommend this study for groups or individuals—for all who need a life changing, fresh dose of hope.

Lori Marshall, Crossline Community Church women's director

Let these psalms come alive afresh within your soul! The authors have masterfully crafted each study to plumb the depths of the biblical text. This guide is unsurpassed by its multitude of creative ways to make these spiritual truths sing within your own spirit passionately and personally.

Bob Kopeny, Calvary Chapel East Anaheim pastor

DISCOVERING HOPE IN THE PSALMS

PAM FARREL & JEAN E. JONES

author &
illustrator **KARLA DORNACHER**

HARVEST HOUSE PUBLISHERS
EUGENE, OREGON

Cover by Dugan Design Group, Bloomington, MN

Cover illustration by Karla Dornacher

Pam Farrel published in association with the literary agency of The Steve Laube Agency, LLC, 24 W. Camelback Rd. A-635, Phoenix, AZ 85013

DISCOVERING HOPE IN THE PSALMS

Copyright © 2017 text by Pam Farrel, Jean E. Jones, and Karla Dornacher.
Illustrations © 2017 by Karla Dornacher
Published by Harvest House Publishers
Eugene, Oregon 97408
www.harvesthousepublishers.com

ISBN 978-0-7369-6997-0 (pbk.)

Printed in the United States of America

20 21 22 23 24 25 / CM-JC / 11 10 9 8 7 6 5

Dedication

In the beginning God CREATED…(Genesis 1:1).

To all those creatives who love to weave the beauty of Scripture with the beauty of art to allow God to create the ultimate loveliness of life-change: May these psalms exquisitely paint your future with hope's splendor.

To all the God-loving artists who bravely pour your heart onto pages, papers, and canvasses when inspired by the Word of God: Thank you.

~All of us

To the God of Hope who inspired the psalmists
to pen poems of magnificent authenticity:
Bless you, this writer is forever grateful.
~ Pam

To Clay, for his incredible love and support
~ Jean E.

To Michael,
who never gave up hope on me even during the darkest hours
~ Karla

Contents

Do You Want Hope?

Do you want the hope that takes you through the dark valleys of life's journey? The world and our lives can seem crazy and disappointing and often dark and despairing: dreams dissolve; cancers ravage; friends betray; loved ones wound; we fail.

The psalmists faced distresses, too, but they cultivated hope by praying psalms of hope and resting in God's promises. Their writings nurture that hope in us today by leading us to God's presence so we experience his mercy in new ways.

Why We Wrote This Discovery Book for You

The three of us, with our different paths and gifts, have connected over our love for interacting with God's Word and encouraging others to experience the hope of his promises and faithfulness.

Our desire to share the riches of hope from Psalms with you is the inspiration behind the creation of this journey. By the end of our time together, you'll know how to pray and hope in dark times and how to rejoice and act wisely at all times. You'll grasp eight hopes from Psalms that will draw you closer to God and will brace you in troubling times. You'll confidently interpret the psalms and hold on to their messages as lifelines.

We can't wait to join you for this adventure.

Jean E.

Twenty years ago the women's ministry director of my church asked me to write a homework-style Bible study on Psalm 71 for a large group of women. I immersed myself in that psalm for months and realized the psalmist knew something I didn't know: how to pray with hope. My prayers were often worry sessions that left me no more peaceful than I was before I prayed.

I wrote my own prayer psalm based on Psalm 71 and realized this activity could benefit everyone. At the time I was a systems analyst writing training materials and teaching computer software, and I knew the benefits of hands-on exercises. So in the study, I walked the women through writing a psalm without telling them what they were doing until they were done. The next time we met, excited chatter filled the room: "Did you get to the last page? Did you realize we were writing our own psalm?" They loved it, and they couldn't wait to share their psalms with each other.

Through that experience I discovered that most people don't know how to pray the psalms and don't realize prayer was the purpose of these amazing writings. That realization became my inspiration to connect with Pam and Karla to guide women into discovering hope in the Psalms through in-depth study, inspiring devotionals, and optional creative experiences designed to help each of us experience Psalms in a new, transforming way.

Pam

The Psalms have always been my inspiration at the critical turning points of my life. One of the first passages I memorized as a child was Psalm 23. Psalm 37 held the confirmation I needed to happily say "Yes!" to marrying my husband, Bill. In times of struggle, doubt, and hopelessness, the Psalms have kept me emotionally afloat.

So when my friend Jean asked me to advise her on her Bible study on the Psalms, I was excited and intrigued. Jean and her husband, Dr. Clay Jones, have been friends and encouragers to our *Love-Wise* ministry for several decades, and I knew of Jean's strong Bible teaching skills. But when I had the wonderful opportunity to read her work, I experienced the power of her ability to help women dig a little deeper to discover gems in the Word. So I championed the creation of this project wholeheartedly.

While I worked my way through the study, I longed to express what I was learning. I enjoy connecting the beauty of art with the beauty of Scripture, so I drew out the rich meanings and applications I was learning in my journaling Bible and in my art journal. I suggested offering the reader a variety of artistic and creative options, and this led to me calling one of my favorite artists, Karla Dornacher, to see if she would create coloring pages to go with these psalms. I know from personal experience that this unique study is life-changing.

Karla

I know what hopelessness looks like. I've walked in that pitch-black tunnel where there was no glimmer of light. More than once, I believed suicide was my only way out of the darkness that imprisoned me.

I grew up with a narcissistic mother and a stepdad who was mentally and emotionally abusive. I ran away from home at 17 only to return the next day, knowing it was wrong. Shortly after that my mother legally disowned me and I became a ward of the state. She refused to speak to me for seven years.

During those years, my constant companions were hurt, confusion, and anger. Pain and strong emotions kept spilling out onto the two people I loved the most: my husband and baby girl. I knew I had problems; there was no hiding it. In a desperate attempt to find hope and a purpose for living, I sought help from all the wrong sources—everything from spiritual gurus to self-help remedies.

In the fall of 1980, I was invited to a neighborhood Bible study, and there I discovered hope: hope in Christ, and hope in his Word. The truths of who God is and who he says I am *in* him brought light into my darkness and slowly began to replace the lies I had believed as a child. I remember the first time I read Psalm 27:10: "For my father and my mother have forsaken me, but the Lord will take me in." And he did. And I had hope.

I soon realized my artistic ability was a gift from God, and I asked him if he would someday allow me to use my art to glorify him and help other women discover his hope. And he has, even now, through this discovery book.

The Treasures in Each Chapter

Your path through every chapter unfolds with an engaging study on one or two psalms of hope. It will also guide you in writing your own prayer psalm and will give you options for creatively immersing yourself in Scripture.

Why? The more ways we immerse ourselves in a passage, the better we'll remember its message. We all have different learning styles, so the tool that works best for you might not be the tool that works best for your closest friend. And we know you'll have a blast trying new creative options and delighting in others' ideas and experiences.

We collaborated on this discovery book to inspire you. Here's what you'll find from each of us in every chapter.

Jean E.

Daily Lessons

You'll hear from me throughout this journey. The opening page of each chapter tells you the hope we'll look at and the key question we'll answer.

Next, the psalm selection we'll study in each chapter is printed for you and is illustrated by Karla. The translation is English Standard Version, but I use indentations, line breaks, and stanza breaks from a variety of scholars to fit our discussions better. Refer to these printed psalms to answer the lesson questions.

After the psalm are the five daily lessons, each answering the key question from the opening page and centering on the hope that the psalm selection gives us in God. Each lesson will take around 25 minutes to complete. The first lesson introduces the psalm's genre and ends with options for creatively experiencing the psalm's hope. The chapter's final lesson on Day 5 will guide you in a private time of worship, using at least three psalms, including your own.

The lessons use three icons:

A quarter note represents a personal question designed to help you apply what you're learning to your life one note at a time. If you're in a small group, your group leader will ask for volunteers to share their answers. The personal questions will promote a rich discussion and help everyone learn and grow from others' experiences.

The beamed notes represent an activity which will walk you through writing a prayer psalm based on the one you're studying. We encourage you to share your finished psalm with your small group and on social media.

An activity marked with a fermata (for sustaining a note further) indicates that additional and relevant instructions, insights, and resources can be found at www.DiscoveringHopeInThePsalms.com. Come visit us there!

The Little Details
Along the way, you'll see sidebars titled "The Little Details." These are extra insights for both seasoned Christians and seekers who thrive on details.

My Psalm
After the five daily lessons, I've added a page—My Psalm—for you to write your own, personal prayer psalm. You can illustrate it and embellish the page any way you wish.

Pam
Hope Alive
My unique contribution is the Hope Alive section in each chapter, where I share honest, personal examples of how studying these psalms has kept hope alive in my own life and how this study will encourage and equip you to hold on to hope. I also offer a bridge to the artist within many of you with my Creative Biblical Expressions. You'll find more examples of these on our website along with more Scripture, more hope, and more art so your journey of knowing God's love can continue long after the pages of this discovery book are read, filled, and colored.

Karla
Creative Connection
You'll hear from me at the end of each chapter in the Creative Connection that follows My Psalm. I'll share inspiration and ideas to help you see God's Word through your own creative lens and express it through your unique artistic talents. You'll be encouraged to use the creative moments you have during this study as opportunities to hear God's heart for you as well as hide his Word in your heart. And you'll discover a few design, coloring, and hand-lettering tips to jump-start your own creative journey through the Psalms.

Illustrations

You'll see my illustrations throughout the discovery book. I designed the full-page graphics at the end of each chapter to give you the opportunity to creatively express yourself with color as well as spend time meditating on God's Word. Use colored pencils or markers to color—just remember to slip a sheet of blank paper behind the page in case your markers bleed through. The bookmarks in the back of the book are for you to cut out and color or slip under a page in your Bible, sketchbook, or gratitude journal for tracing. Look for tracing tips and other helps in the Creative Connection sections.

From All of Us

At the end of each chapter's first daily lesson, we list ideas on how to creatively express the psalm you're studying and the hope it gives you. These become ways to meditate on the psalm's message throughout the time you work through each chapter and to share your hope and experience with others. Choose any that interest you, or come up with your own. Of course, if the creative options aren't your thing, that's okay too!

To help you memorize Scripture, we have provided the Tips for Committing Scripture to Heart section at the end of the book's primary content. What a gift it is to have the hopes in Psalms treasured in your mind, heart, and spirit. We encourage you to try each of the ideas once so you can discover the method that works the best for you. And if you have personal methods for memorizing Scripture, share those with us and other readers at the Discovering Hope in the Psalms Facebook group.

Our website, www.DiscoveringHopeInThePsalms.com, has even more ideas and instructions, along with links to help you share your creative projects and gather inspiration from others.

How to Use *Discovering Hope in the Psalms*

This discovery book is designed for both small groups and individual study.

Ideas for Small Groups

Begin with an introductory meeting where you hand out discovery books, go over what to expect, and provide time for everyone to introduce themselves. Use icebreakers such as these:

- Which creative hobbies have you tried or enjoyed?
- Does the idea of having creative options in this study sound scary or exciting?
- How have you used creativity as (a) a conversation starter; (b) a means to share the gospel; or (c) a way to encourage someone?
- Do you draw in your Bible? Why or why not?
- Describe a time in your life when you needed hope.
- Name one thing in the news that discourages you.
- What area of your life needs the healing of hope?
- Name one benefit you hope to embrace during this study.

Each time you meet, carve out time to worship with psalms in song or spoken-word poetry. Consider providing demonstrations of ways to creatively interact with psalms. Ask for volunteers or bring in artists for a special event.

For the final meeting, consider having a potluck so participants can bring gifts of food to share as they read one of the thanksgiving prayers they wrote. Set aside time for participants to share creative projects they've finished but have not yet shared.

Nine-Week Option

One way to go through the lessons is to cover one chapter a week. The first week, begin with an introductory meeting. During each of the following eight weeks, discuss the personal questions and a few key questions from all five daily lessons of one chapter. Encourage participants to share their psalms and the creative endeavors they've begun.

Seventeen-Week Option

To extend your group's time of exploration, you could cover one chapter every two weeks. Begin with the introductory meeting and end with a potluck at the last meeting. For instance, participants could complete three daily lessons and begin a creative project the first week, and the second week complete the final two lessons and their psalm, and continue with their creative project. The first discussion centers on the three lessons and the projects begun, while the second discussion finishes the lessons and gives everyone time to share their prayer psalm and progress on creative projects. Those who want to can explore other psalms of the same genre (usually listed in a Day 1 sidebar).

Inspiration for Individual Study

You can work through the lessons at your own pace, spending as much or as little time as you'd like on the creative options. We encourage you to share your creative endeavors on social media so you benefit from the community you'll find there. You're not in this journey alone, even if you decide to do this as an independent study. Visit us through the links at www.DiscoveringHopeInThePsalms.com so we can see your creations and answer your questions. We have come alongside you for this journey of hope and would love to keep in touch.

Are you ready to join us in discovering hope in the psalms? Turn the page and let's get started!

Jean F. Pam Karla

Chapter 1

Psalm 1:
The Hope of God's Blessing

What should I do to have a blessed life?

Day 1

Introducing the Book of Psalms

Would you like to be like a tree planted by streams of water that yields fruit in its season and whose leaf does not wither? Would you like to prosper in all that you do?

We'll learn how as we start our journey of hope in Psalms. First, let's explore how this amazing book of the Bible came into being and why it is so inspiring.

Hebrew poets penned the praises and prayers they worshiped God with as psalms. Psalms are poems meant to be sung, so the poets at times gave their psalms to the temple choirmasters. The choirmasters gathered the psalms into collections. What we know today as the book of Psalms is a collection of these collections.

For thousands of years, followers of God have worshiped him by singing and praying the psalms in the Psalter, as the book of Psalms is also known. It's no wonder. The Psalms extol God's goodness and power. They voice our gratitude and hopes, our sorrows and longings. When we sing or pray them, they teach us eternal truths and commit us to godly actions and attitudes. They draw us near to God.

And there's more.

Although worship is our gift to God, when we worship with psalms, something happens within us: Hope soars, and we are transformed. The psalms proclaim the hopes to which we have been called, and in our attempts to bless the living God, we find ourselves blessed.

In this first chapter we will look at a psalm that places before us the **hope of blessing.** It answers the question, *What should I do to have a blessed life?* Take a moment to ask the Lord to speak to you through his Word, and then read Psalm 1 printed for you on the next page.[1]

> Although worship is our gift to God, when we worship with psalms, something happens within us: Hope soars, and we are transformed.

Psalm 1

1   Blessed is the man
        who walks not in the counsel of the wicked,
        nor stands in the way of sinners,
        nor sits in the seat of scoffers;
2   But his delight is in the law of the Lord,
        and on his law he meditates day and night.
3   He is like a tree planted by streams of water
        that yields its fruit in its season
            and its leaf does not wither.
        In all that he does, he prospers.

4   The wicked are not so,
        but are like chaff that the wind drives away.
5   Therefore the wicked will not stand in the judgment,
        nor sinners in the congregation of the righteous;

6   for the Lord knows the way of the righteous,
        but the way of the wicked will perish.

Initial Thoughts

1. 🎵 What stands out to you most from your initial reading of this psalm?

The Big Picture

Just as today we hear many types of songs—love songs, anthems, lullabies, ballads, and more—so the ancient Hebrews heard many types of psalms—wisdom songs, laments, thanksgiving songs, hymns, confidence songs, royal psalms, and more. Knowing a psalm's type helps us to know how to read it.

Psalm 1 is a **wisdom psalm** written to instruct us in God's ways.[2] This particular type of wisdom psalm is called a **Torah psalm**, a psalm that extols God's instructions to us. (*Torah* means "law" or "instructions.")

Psalm 1 tells us what to do to have a blessed life. Being *blessed* isn't quite the same as being happy; it's "the joyful spiritual condition of those who are right with God and the pleasure and satisfaction that is derived from that."[3]

The psalm contrasts the ways of two types of people.

2. Who are these people, according to the psalm's concluding verse (Psalm 1:6)?

Psalm 1 introduces the first of the two main themes of the Psalter: the way of the righteous. But what do the psalms mean by "righteous"? The Bible uses the term *righteous* in several ways. It tells us the standard for righteousness is God's righteousness, and that no person is righteous on his or her own. However, Scripture calls some people *the righteous*: those whose faith in and love for God causes them to order their lives according to God's laws (Psalm 1:2). God bestows righteousness on them because he counts faith as righteousness. In the New Testament, God makes righteous those who put their faith in Jesus. In both the Old and New Testaments, the righteous aren't sinless, but when they sin, they seek God's forgiveness, and God cleanses them of unrighteousness (more on this in chapter 3).

Beeson Divinity School professor of Old Testament and Hebrew, Allen P. Ross, puts it this way:

> The basic meaning of "righteous" has to do with conforming to the standard; in religious passages that standard is divine revelation. The righteous are people who have entered into covenant with God by faith and seek to live according to his Word. The covenant that they have makes them the people of God—God knows them, and because God knows them, they shall never perish. They may do unrighteous things at times, but they know to find forgiveness because they want to do what is right.[4]

The wicked, on the other hand, are those who live as they see fit. The word translated

The Little Details
Stanzas

In poetry, a **stanza** is a group of related poetic lines. It's similar to a paragraph, which in prose is a group of related sentences. Some modern Bible translations break psalms into stanzas to make them easier to read.

Psalm 1's first stanza (verses 1-3) describes the righteous, the second (verses 4-5) describes the wicked, and the last (verse 6) draws a conclusion about the two.

Scripture calls some people *the righteous*: those whose faith in and love for God causes them to order their lives according to God's laws.

The Little Details

Psalms: A Collection of Collections

The Bible's book of Psalms is actually five books of psalms collected over 1000 years.[7] Moses wrote its oldest psalm around 1400 BC. David, who reigned around 1000 BC, authored more of its psalms than anyone else. Some psalms date to around the time of Ezra—approximately 400 BC.

It was about 400 BC when compilers arranged the Psalter into the form we have today, placing Psalms 1 and 2 as its introduction. Together they announce the two major themes threading throughout the Psalter: the way of the righteous and the rule of the divinely appointed king.

wicked in Psalm 1:1 can refer to those who simply don't love God, or to those who reject God's laws,[5] or even to those dedicated to violence and oppression.

3. In the following verses, underline what both the Old and New Testaments tell us about our ability to be righteous without God's help.

   No one living is righteous before you (Psalm 143:2).

   None is righteous, no, not one (Romans 3:10).

4. Why can't we be righteous on our own (Romans 3:23)?

5. (a) In Matthew 22:37-38 below, underline the command that those without faith in God always break. (b) Circle what Jesus called that command.

   And [Jesus] said to him, "You shall love the Lord your God with all your heart and with all your soul and with all your mind. This is the great and first commandment."

6. Underline what the righteousness from God comes through in Philippians 3:9 below:

   ...not having a righteousness of my own that comes from the law, but that which comes through faith in Christ, the righteousness from God that depends on faith.

When reading Scripture, it's important to differentiate between righteous living—ordering one's life by God's commands, including the command to love God—and righteous standing—the righteousness God gives people who live by faith.

Righteous living without faith is simply keeping a moral code and never leads to righteous standing because no person is sinless and because God gives righteous standing to only those with faith in him (Romans 3:20,23). Remember, those without faith in God always break the greatest command: Love the Lord your God.

On the other hand, righteous standing always leads to righteous living because those with faith in God love and trust him enough to obey him (albeit imperfectly on earth), and because God works in them to change them.[6] It may take time to overcome weaknesses and old habits, but the Holy Spirit will produce growth.

7. Read Luke 6:46-49. (a) What question does Jesus ask in verse 46? (b) How would you reply? (c) Summarize what Jesus says about righteous living (that is, doing what he says) in verses 47-49.

According to Jesus, we must build our lives on the foundation of obeying his words if we want to be blessed. Those who call him "Lord, Lord" but don't obey him are building a house without a foundation, and that house will fall. It's a different analogy with the same message.

Experiencing Psalm 1 Creatively

Throughout this series, we'll introduce you to a variety of ways to interpret psalms using creative biblical expressions. Some of these may be new to you.

The arts played a big part in Israel's worship of God, including visual, performing, literary, and even culinary arts. Experiencing Scripture through multiple means helps plant its message in us so we can remember its truths even better than if we just read it. It also gives us more ways to draw near to God in worship.

Below you'll find ideas for engaging with psalms using the various arts. Mark any that interest you and consider doing at least one in the weeks to come. A few are specifically for engaging with Psalm 1, but most will work for any psalm. Find instructions for items marked ⊙ at www.DiscoveringHopeInThePsalms.com.

Visual Arts Options

- Find techniques for expressing Scripture with art in Karla's Creative Connection at the end of each chapter.
- Color Karla's full-page illustration at the end of each chapter.
- The bookmark on the opening page of each chapter is reproduced at the end of the book. Color and cut it out for yourself or to give it as a gift.
- For this chapter's psalm, Psalm 1, create a container garden with a small plant pruned like a tree and tiny rocks suggesting a stream. Use this as a conversation starter and as a visual inspiration for your personal time of prayer and study.
- Write part or all of a psalm in calligraphy.
- Create an art journal: sketch, paint, and affix photos and words from magazines.
- ⊙ Overlay a verse on top of a photograph.
- Create a diorama, sculpture, or piece of jewelry.
- Create fabric art using cross-stitch, embroidery, or appliqué.
- ⊙ Scan the bookmark, use photo editing software to color it, and print it on printable fabric to use as is or to embroider.
- Create greeting cards or T-shirts to encourage others.
- ⊙ In a journaling Bible, choose one verse to illuminate in the wide margin.

Performing Arts Options

- ⊙ Find a musical version of the psalm to play or sing.
- Act out the psalm as you read or recite it aloud to music (spoken-word poetry).
- Write music and lyrics based on the psalm.
- If a psalm tells you to do something, do it!

The Little Details
Visual Arts

In biblical times, Scripture adorned the doorposts and gates of homes, providing teaching opportunities. But where the visual arts really stood out was at the temple. There, wood carvings, gold inlays, intricate embroidery, and bronze statues reminded worshipers that this was the temple of the Creator of all in heaven and earth. He was holy, and they drew near to him through sacrifice. The artistry reminded people who God was so they could worship appropriately.

Literary Arts Options

- Form a psalm's message into a poem of any type you like.
- Write an encouraging letter to someone based on the hope you find in the psalm.
- 👁 Write a wisdom psalm similar to what you're studying, using what you learn about Hebrew poetry. Here's an example of such a psalm based on Ephesians 4:29,31.

> Blessed are those
> > who whisper not secrets about friends,
> > nor murmur rumors about acquaintances,
> > nor shout lies about foes.
>
> But they delight in building up others,
> > and on ways to give grace they ponder.
>
> They are like master craftsmen with fine tools
> > who repair and strengthen weak fittings,
> > > and wipe away grime that hides beauty.
> > In all their relationships they prosper.
>
> Gossipers are not so,
> > but are like vandals who mar and destroy.
>
> Therefore gossipers will not keep close companions,
> > nor slanderers the trust of the wise.
>
> For the Lord brings friends to encouragers,
> > but the friendships of the slanderer will collapse.

Culinary Arts Options

- Celebrate a Christian holiday with a feast, where you talk about the meaning of the holiday.
- Celebrate answered prayer with a meal, where you publicly give thanks (more on this in Chapter 8).

Sharing Options

- Share your creations with your small group.
- 👁 To inspire others, post recordings, writings, and pictures in the Facebook group Discovering Hope in the Psalms.
- Also share on Facebook, Instagram, and Twitter with #DiscoveringHopeInThePsalms.

Hope Alive

We all want to be blessed by God, right? But do we desire to place ourselves in line to receive the blessing? Psalm 1 begins with that word we all deep down hope for: *blessed*. We long for the fruit of being blessed; and we hope to be a tree that "yields fruit" and to "prosper" in all that we do. Verse 2 reveals the key that unlocks such blessing is that "his [or her] delight is in the law of the LORD, and on his law he meditates day and night."

When people ask me how I have overcome traumatic family-of-origin issues or how my husband, Bill, and I have formed a lasting love and parented with creativity, my response is the same: "The power is in the Word." I share how I dig into the Bible daily. I admit that I struggle to memorize Scripture, but I keep at it because it's life-changing. God wants us to delight in our journey to the blessing with our focus on him.

A friend and I recently hiked five miles up a mountain to take photos on the famous Potato Chip Rock in California. Our push to the top unveiled inspiring, snapshot-worthy views of lakes, rock formations, the valley, and the distant Pacific Ocean shore. I was equally encouraged by the deep conversations I had with my friend. Precious memories were made not only at the peak, but along the trail.

In the same way, God gave me personal gems along my journey through these psalms, even though I've studied them many times before. This time through Psalm 1, I pondered what it would mean in my life to be a tree planted by streams of water with a leaf that never withers. Following the research trail, I discovered the "streams" mentioned are irrigation canals common in the Middle East. Fruit trees, especially the nutritious and delicious date palms, were planted near these waterways to ensure prosperity. I conducted word studies on *tree*, *planted*, *yields fruit*, and *prosper*. I responded to God with prayer and praise. I penned a poem in my own psalmist-like way. I prayerfully savored the fruit of these studies on walks down my tree-lined driveway. I sketched a tree with deep roots. In short, I sat in the shade of this Psalm 1 tree and reflected on my own life.

Then, in God's perfect timing, a tree on our property fell. A strong wind or a raging storm didn't topple it. No, the cause was a beetle that can do its damage only in drought conditions. In California, we've been on strict water rationing because of a nearly decade-long drought. The tree appeared healthy, but because of lack of water, it was dead inside. It was a vivid reminder of what kind of tree I did *not* want to become! And "living water"— and lots of it—would be the difference!

Turn on the soaker hose, pull out the sprinklers, and get out your watering can by reading, memorizing, worshiping with, meditating on, and creatively responding to the psalms God is placing along your path. This study will deepen the roots of your life and help you find and hang on to hope. As you trek through the forest of verses, make note of the towering evergreen trees (you and other students of the Word) made strong by the streams of study. We know you will enjoy the journey up to the mountain peak of HOPE. Take it from a fellow explorer: You will love the view from up top!

Pam

Day 2

Two Ways

I wasn't raised in church. A girlfriend gave me my first Bible when I was a high school freshman: a *Good News for Modern Man* paperback New Testament illustrated with striking line drawings. I read it carefully, putting my faith in Jesus as Savior while reading the Gospel of John.

As I continued reading, I realized the way it said people should live was quite different from the way I had been raised. I felt as if I'd finally been given the proper instruction manual for living.

I set out to learn God's instructions and discard the mistaken notions I'd relied on from intuition and the advice of family and friends unfamiliar with God's ways. I didn't know it then, but I was doing what the writer of Psalm 1 describes: delighting in God's instructions.

The Way to Avoid

Psalm 1 tells us whose advice to ignore and whose to follow if we want a blessed life.

> **8.** What three things should a person shun to be blessed (Psalm 1:1)?

The psalms are easier to understand if we know a little about Hebrew poetry. A Hebrew poem's basic unit is a **poetic line**. Most lines have two segments, although some have three or four and a few have only one. In the psalms printed in this workbook, the first segment starts at the left margin and the rest of the segments are indented to show their relationships.

Most line segments in Hebrew poetry use **parallelism.** They say something similar in multiple ways, giving us different ways to grasp the poet's meaning. The best part about parallelism is that it translates well, so we don't have to know Hebrew to enjoy it. God was planning ahead when he helped the Hebrews develop their poetry!

Here are the parallel elements of Psalm 1:1 lined up:

a	Blessed is the man		
b	who walks not	in the counsel	of the wicked
c	nor stands	in the way	of sinners
d	nor sits	in the seat	of scoffers

Notice that I've labeled the line segments *a–d*. Throughout this discovery book, if I place a letter after a verse number, I'm referring to a particular line segment. For example, "Psalm 1:1c" refers to the third line segment: "nor stands in the way of sinners."

When you find parallelism, compare the parallel elements to see how they relate. In this case, they intensify.

First, contact with the corrupt group progresses from walking with, to standing with, to

---

I felt as if I'd finally been given the proper instruction manual for living.

sitting with. Next, involvement progresses from listening to their advice, to following their advice, to becoming one of them. The third intensification depends on the meaning of the word *wicked* in segment 1b. If by *wicked* the psalmist means "ungodly," then the progression is from the ungodly, who lack faith in God; to sinners, who habitually go against God's will; to scoffers, who scorn God-followers, mock the law, and shun correction.

But if he means the violent and oppressive, then the progression follows what we do when we're enticed. We begin by listening to those who act wickedly. Then we step into sin as we tell ourselves, "At least I'm not as bad as they are." But later we become enmeshed in the same deeds, and then it's a small move to scoffing at all who don't do likewise.

The Way to Take

The psalmist next moves from the way to avoid to the way to take.

> 9. What are the two ways the righteous respond to the law of the Lord (Psalm 1:2)?

The word translated *law* is *Torah*. It could also be translated *instructions*. The "law of the Lord" includes all of God's instructions to us in Scripture,[8] for Scripture is "breathed out by God" for our benefit (2 Timothy 3:16-17).

Let's look more closely at verse 2.

> 10. (a) In verse 2 below, circle "his delight is" in segment 2a and "he meditates" in segment 2b. Draw a line between the two circles. (b) Draw a box around "in the law of the Lord" in 2a and "on his law" in 2b. Now draw a line between the two boxes.
>
> But his delight is in the law of the Lord,
>
> and on his law he meditates day and night.

Notice how your two lines form an *X*? Like verse 1, verse 2 uses parallelism, but this time the parallel elements are placed in a pattern called **chiasm** (KEY-asm; *chi* is the Greek name for the letter *X*). We illustrate verse 2's parallelism like this:

A   his delight is

   B   in the law of the Lord

   B′   on his law

A′   he meditates

The righteous so delight in the Lord's instructions that they meditate on them all the time.

The Little Details

Poetic Lines

A **poetic line** is not the same as a sentence. Lines can have multiple sentences (such as verse 3), and a single sentence might be made up of multiple lines (such as verses 1-2). A line is not the same as a verse, either. Sometimes our modern verse numbers don't correspond to a psalm's poetic lines.

Just as Bible versions sometimes differ as to where they put sentence and paragraph breaks, so they sometimes differ as to where they put line and stanza breaks.

Line Indentations

Your Bible may indent Psalm 1 differently than we do in this discovery book. Many Bible versions place the first line segment at the left margin and indent the rest of the segments about one-quarter inch. A third level of indention, to about one-half inch, means the line was too long to fit within the margins so it wraps.

Since this discovery book has wider text than most Bibles, it can display multiple levels of indents where called for while avoiding line wraps, so I show more levels of indent.

The Little Details
Parallelism

We can symbolize parallelism by using letters to represent units and a **prime mark** (′) to show how many times a unit has been repeated.

Normal parallelism (verse 5):

A B / A′ B′

Incomplete parallelism (verse 1):

A / B C D / B′ C′ D′ / B″ C″ D″

Chiastic parallelism (verse 2):

A B / B′ A′

We naturally think about what delights us.

We naturally think about what delights us. Delight brings meditation, and meditation increases delight.

The Hebrew word translated *meditates* has a broader meaning than our English word. Meditation includes pondering God's instructions, devising ways to follow them, and saying the commands aloud quietly. The word is often translated *utter* or *mutter*. Isaiah used it to describe doves cooing (Isaiah 38:14) and a lion growling over its prey (Isaiah 31:4). This last reference provides an apt image: As a lion growls over the prey he devours, refusing to abandon it to the shepherds who attempt to scare him off, so we should utter God's words as we devour them, refusing to abandon them to mockers.

11. (a) According to Joshua 1:8, what is the goal of meditating on God's instructions? (b) What blessing would then follow? (c) Can we obey God if we don't know what he wants us to do? (d) Can we obey if we don't meditate on how well our lives correlate to God's instructions? Explain.

12. ◖ How can you delight yourself in God's instructions?

13. Look back at Psalm 1. Complete the following chart by comparing the wicked in verse 1 with the righteous in verse 2. (Remember, the letters *a*, *b*, *c*, and *d* refer to line segments within the verse.) The first line is filled in for you.

	Wicked	Righteous
Source of counsel	1b: *The wicked*	2a: *The law of the LORD*
Practices	1c:	2b:
Attitude toward God's will	1d:	2a:

Jesus taught something similar: "Blessed rather are those who hear the word of God and keep it!" (Luke 11:28).

Salvation is not found through obeying God's laws. No one but Jesus has ever lived a sinless life, and salvation is purely a gift from God. But obeying God brings blessings, both because God watches over and blesses those who obey him even when it costs them and because God's laws are laws of love and living according to them brings blessings in itself.

How often I've watched the truth of this borne out in my life and in the lives of those I know. Couples who made forgiving an essential part of marriage grew closer, while those who held grudges broke apart. Friends committed to honesty matured spiritually, while those who hid sins behind lies stagnated. Gossipers lost friendships, while those who built up others gained friends.

14. ♪ (a) What's an instruction from God that you've seen bring blessing to people's lives? (b) How do those who follow this instruction bless others? (c) How are they themselves blessed by following this instruction? (d) Without using names, what are ways you've seen people hindered by not following this same instruction?

Psalm 1 describes the importance of meditating on God's words. Let's write a simple psalm that will help us prayerfully meditate on Psalm 1. We'll write four stanzas, each using a specific type of prayer: praising, confessing, asking, and thanking. Don't worry about how "good" your words are—the goal isn't to be as eloquent as our psalmist but to worship God from your heart by proclaiming truths about his words.

15. ♫ Read Psalm 1 again while watching for what it says about God's character and his care for you. (a) Turn to the My Psalm page at the end of the chapter and write your name to the right of "A Psalm of." (b) Below the word "Praising," write a line or two praising God's character.

There! We've begun a psalm that we'll finish by the end of this chapter. On Day 3 we'll conclude the psalmist's description of the righteous person and then move on to how he describes the wicked.

The Little Details
Literary Arts

Moses, Miriam, and other men and women in the Bible wrote songs for others to sing so they would remember God's instructions and mighty deeds. At least one shepherd boy, David, wrote psalms for use in personal worship. Later, worship leaders wrote psalms to be sung by the choirs and recited by the masses. Some wrote histories and testimonies to teach others about God. Church leaders wrote letters to encourage, admonish, and bless.

- - - - - - - - - - - - - - - - - - -

Worship God from your heart by proclaiming truths about his words.

- - - - - - - - - - - - - - - - - - -

Day 3

Two Comparisons

The psalmists often paint word pictures to help us understand them. In the next two verses, **imagery** vividly displays the righteous and the wicked.

> **16.** Read Psalm 1:3-4. (a) In one word, what are those who delight in the Lord's instructions like? (b) What about those who scoff at the Lord's commands?

A Well-Watered Fruit Tree

The psalms are rich in images common to ancient Israelites, but some are not so familiar to today's reader accustomed to modern conveniences and different climates. To understand the imagery of Psalm 1, we need to know what ancient Palestine was like and the significance of trees and chaff then.

The Palestinian climate is arid, with a five-month dry season (mid-May to mid-October) followed by a seven-month rainy season. In some areas, temperatures are high during the dry season but mild during the rainy season. The months during which the two seasons transition bring scorching east winds that whip dust clouds and wither plants. Because of this, in ancient times land was often treeless except near springs, rivers, and manmade canals.[9]

A well-watered tree that could withstand hot, dry seasons and withering east winds provided people and animals with dependable food, shade, and protection, and birds with a place to live (Daniel 4:12).

> **17.** (a) What is the person who delights in God's instruction like (Psalm 1:3a)? (b) What does the tree yield seasonally that benefits people and animals (1:3b)?

How does this relate to us? Followers of God bear fruit in at least two ways. We bear spiritual fruit as we grow more like Christ (Galatians 5:22-23), and we bear fruit in good works (Colossians 1:9-10).

> **18.** (a) What else is significant about the tree (Psalm 1:3c)? (b) Why was that important? (Hint: Glance back at the introduction to this section.)

Life is hard, and much in it can cause us to wither if we do not have our roots drinking deeply of God's words.[10] Having deep roots that constantly draw in the water of God's words gives us shady leaves that don't wither and that can help others seeking respite from the scorching sun of hardship.

In the line's final segment, the psalmist explains the tree imagery.

> **19.** (a) The tree just described is important, valuable, and beneficial. What does this tell us about the person who is like this tree? (b) What happens to this person (Psalm 1:3d)?

The psalmist doesn't mean nothing will ever go wrong or nothing will be hard for people who follow God; in fact, plenty of psalms address hardships befalling godly people. But living God's way results in better relationships and better success overall.

As a tree flourishes when it draws in water, so we flourish when we draw in God's instructions. Just as a tree withers when it stops drawing in water, so we wither when we stop drawing in God's words.

Wind-Blown Chaff

The psalmist now describes the wicked, beginning with another word picture. This one is of chaff at harvest.

Chaff is the worthless husks and stalks that have to be separated from grain. In ancient times, after farmers harvested grains, they threshed it by beating or trampling it to separate the grain from its husk. Winnowers then tossed the crushed stalks into the air with winnowing forks, allowing the wind to blow away the lighter chaff while the heavier grain dropped to the ground.

> **20.** (a) What is the wicked person like (Psalm 1:4)? (b) What does a light breeze do to chaff? (c) How does that differ from what the scorching east wind does to a well-watered tree? (d) Compare the value of chaff to that of a fruitful tree.

God calls us to be fruitful. Those who shun God and refuse that calling lack eternal value (Matthew 7:19; 25:30).

Take a look at how the Gospels build on this figure of speech.

> **21.** What did John the Baptist say about Jesus (Matthew 3:12)?

The Little Details
Imagery and Similes

The psalmists paint many word pictures. They use such **imagery** to describe difficult abstract concepts in a way that touches our emotions and helps us understand multiple layers of meaning through mental images.

The imagery in Psalm 1:3 is called a **simile**. A simile is a comparison between two different things that uses the word *like* or the word *as* to describe a similarity: "He is *like* a tree." When a simile grows into a story, it's called a **parable.**

The book of Psalms contains many similes but no parables in this sense. Jesus, however, often spoke in parables, and his parable of the barren fig tree in Luke 13:6-9 has similarities to Psalm 1.

Life is hard, and much in it can cause us to wither if we do not have our roots drinking deeply of God's words.

The Little Details
Culinary Arts

Worship included feasts with elements that often symbolized an aspect of God's care. For example, the spring Passover feast included lamb to represent the Passover lamb slain that they might live, and unleavened bread to signify how hastily the people fled Egypt (Exodus 12:39). Thanksgiving celebrations included a feast for friends, family, priests, and the poor.

John refers here to the end of the age when Jesus will send the angels to separate the unrighteous from the righteous as winnowers separate chaff from wheat.

22. ♩ What can you do this week to be like the tree drinking deeply of the water streams nearby?

Let's write the next two stanzas of your psalm.

23. ♪ Read Psalm 1 while considering if it convicts you of anything you want to confess and turn from. (a) Turn to the My Psalm page. Beneath the word "Confessing," write a line confessing what convicts you and expressing your desire to change. Omit personal details. (b) Write a line thanking God for forgiving you because Jesus died to pay for your sins.

24. ♪ Read Psalm 1 again while looking for one thing it challenges you to do. (a) On the My Psalm page beneath the word "Asking," write a line asking God to help you do this. (b) Write a line expressing why you want to do this.

Two Destinies

The half wall that borders our backyard patio hides a small vegetable garden. The plants growing there have one of two destinies: table or trash can.

Their destinies differ because some serve the purpose for which I prepared the garden, and others do not. Those that hinder the well-being and health of those that do serve the purpose can't stay. Weeds and the neighbor's morning glories that wander over our wall go into the garbage. So do edibles that don't thrive. But the arugula, chard, crookneck squash, and serrano peppers that do well make it to my table.

Psalm 1 tells us people likewise have two destinies.

> **25.** Read Psalm 1:5-6. (a) Who will be separated from whom (verse 5)? (b) What will happen to the wicked (verse 6)?

The Destinies of the Wicked and the Righteous

Psalm 1:5 continues the second stanza's description of the wicked.

> **26.** In what two places will those who reject God and his ways not stand (Psalm 1:5)?

Here, "the wicked" and "sinners" are different words to describe the same people. Because verse 4 talks about separating the wicked from the righteous, the judgment verse 5 refers to is probably the final judgment.

> **27.** In Psalm 76:7 below, underline what makes some unable to stand before God's judgment.
>
> But you, you are to be feared! Who can stand before you when once your anger is roused?

Let's look more at the final judgment.

The Little Details

Types of Parallelism

Here are common types of parallelism and examples of verses that use them.

In **synonymous parallelism**, the parallel units use **synonyms** (words with similar meanings) to express the same idea in a similar way ("wicked" and "sinners" in verse 5).

In **antithetical parallelism**, the parallel units use **antonyms** (words with opposite meanings) to contrast ideas ("way of the righteous" and "way of the wicked" in verse 6).

In **synthetic parallelism**, the units do something else, such as complete a thought ("are not so" and "are like chaff" in verse 4).

28. (a) According to Jesus, a time will come when the dead will hear his voice and come out of their tombs. Jesus will separate them into two groups, each with a different destiny. To what two places will they go (John 5:28-29)? (b) Back up a few verses. Who has eternal life (5:24)? (c) Stay in verse 24. Into what do they not come? (d) Where have they passed?

D. A. Carson (research professor of New Testament at Trinity Evangelical Divinity School) explains it this way: "The believer does not come to the final judgment, but leaves the court already acquitted."[11] Those who hear Jesus' words and believe God's words have eternal life. They won't perish in the judgment but are among those made righteous.

The psalmist has finished describing the righteous and the wicked, and moves on to his conclusion in the final, one-verse stanza.

The Conclusion

The end of the age will be very different for those who reject God and those who embrace him. Psalm 1:6 tells us why in a chiasm where the parallel units contrast:

A   for the LORD knows

      B   the way of the righteous

      B′   but the way of the wicked

A′   will perish

The word translated *knows* has a broader meaning than our English word, so some Bible translations prefer *watches over*. The word means a type of knowing beyond mere awareness, a knowing that includes intimacy and care. In this verse, the parallel elements contrast; since "the way of the righteous" contrasts with "the way of the wicked," then "knows" contrasts with "will perish." It's a knowing that keeps us from perishing—it saves.[12]

A look at two other verses that use this word will help us understand it.

29. (a) Underline what the Lord knows in Psalm 37:18 below; circle what that knowing results in. (b) Underline whom the Lord knows in Nahum 1:7 below; circle what he is to them.

The LORD knows the days of the blameless, and their heritage will remain forever (Psalm 37:18).

The LORD is good, a stronghold in the day of trouble; he knows those who take refuge in him (Nahum 1:7).

In these verses the Lord knows the blameless (those who have their sins forgiven through faith) and those who take refuge in him (an act of faith). In both verses, knowing a person involves keeping the person safe.

"The believer does not come to the final judgment, but leaves the court already acquitted."
D. A. Carson

Years later, Jesus talked about knowing his own.

30. (a) In John 10:14 below, underline whom Jesus says he knows. (b) In John 10:11, circle what Jesus does for those he knows.

> I am the good shepherd. I know my own and my own know me (John 10:14).
>
> I am the good shepherd. The good shepherd lays down his life for the sheep (John 10:11).

31.  What encouragement do you take from understanding that the Lord knows and watches over the way of his own?

Those who reject the Lord have no such favor.

32. According to Psalm 1:6b, what will perish?

Their way isn't kept safe; it will perish. There are two destinies: The way of the righteous leads to one; the way of the wicked to the other.

Let's write your psalm's final stanza.

33. 🎵 Read Psalm 1 and find at least one thing for which you are thankful. Turn to the My Psalm page and write one or two lines thanking God for this beneath the heading "Thanking."

You've now finished your psalm!

You've also practiced a type of meditative prayer (praising, confessing, asking, thanking) you can use every time you read Scripture. Doing so will develop a habit of meditating, and it will help your hope in God soar because it will inspire you to rely on who God is even as it encourages you to become like him.

The Little Details
Performing Arts

Members of three choirs greeted worshipers at the temple's gates, played music, and sang throughout the temple facility. Men and women alike wrote and sang songs commemorating God's mighty works. All the people acted out important historical events: For Passover, families dressed and feasted the way the Israelites did on the night God freed them from Egyptian slavery, and for the Feast of Tabernacles, they lived in palm booths for a week to reenact the wilderness experience and entering the Promised Land.

Two Words

Today we'll finish looking at Psalm 1. Then we'll close in a special time of worship.

The Beginning and the End

Hebrew poems often repeat something at the end of a poem from the beginning of a poem, a technique called **enclosure**. Enclosure brings us back around to where we started while inviting us to compare the repeated elements.

> **34.** (a) Where does the righteous person not stand (Psalm 1:1)? (b) What perishes (1:6)? (c) Why, then, is it good that the righteous not stand there? (d) Where will the wicked not stand (1:5)?

Those whose master is the Lord, however, will stand: "He will be upheld, for the Lord is able to make him stand" (Romans 14:4).

The first and last words of a poem often have special meaning. Psalm 1's first word begins with the first letter of the Hebrew alphabet, *'aleph*, and its last word begins with the last letter of the Hebrew alphabet, *taw*. This symbolizes totality and completion.[13]

> **35.** What are the first and last words of Psalm 1 in English?

The first and last words are clues to the psalm's theme: There is a way that is blessed and a way that perishes. Wisdom chooses the way of blessing.

As the introduction to the Psalter, Psalm 1 tells us how to enter the Psalter: Walk in the way that is blessed by delighting yourself in the Lord's instructions.

> **36.** 🎵 What elements of this psalm are most encouraging to you today? Why?

Using Psalms in Worship

The apostle Paul describes worship that pleases God in Romans 12:1-2:

> I appeal to you therefore, brothers, by the mercies of God, to present your bodies as a living sacrifice, holy and acceptable to God, which is your spiritual

The first and last words of a poem often have special meaning.

worship. Do not be conformed to this world, but be transformed by the renewal of your mind, that by testing you may discern what is the will of God, what is good and acceptable and perfect.

Our sacrifice of ourselves is a *living sacrifice*—it continues until our earthly lives end. It is *holy*—we keep ourselves separate from what is profane and we dedicate ourselves to the Lord's service. It is *acceptable*—it is the sacrifice that pleases God.[14]

Offering ourselves like this is our *spiritual worship*. Our inner selves—our hearts and minds—fully engage.[15] Such worship requires us to refuse to conform to this world's standards, but to instead be *transformed by the renewal of our minds*.

Now here's the irony: When we worship God with the psalms, the psalms transform our minds. God wants us to offer him transformation as worship, but the very act of worshiping with Psalms is itself transforming.

How? Old Testament professor Gordon Wenham explains one way (we will see more in coming chapters):

> [W]hat worshipers say in prayer ought to have a profound effect on them because these words are addressed to God, who can evaluate their sincerity and worthiness. If we praise a certain type of behavior in our prayers, we are telling God that this is how we intend to behave. On the other hand, if in prayer we denounce certain acts and pray for God to punish them, we are in effect inviting God to judge us if we do the same…[O]ne can listen to a proverb or a story and then take it or leave it, but if you pray ethically, you commit yourself to a path of action.[16]

If we merely read Psalm 1, we will not engage with it as fully as if we worship with it. If we worship with Psalm 1 by praying or singing it to God, then we commit to not walking in the counsel of the wicked, and thus we commit to not being conformed to this world. We instead delight in and meditate on God's instructions so we will be transformed into that fruitful tree whose leaf withers not.

And then we will discern the good and acceptable and perfect will of God—and our offering of ourselves will be living, holy, and acceptable to God.

Worshiping with Torah Psalms

At the end of each chapter, we'll spend some time worshiping God with psalms. This time will be most meaningful and worshipful if you prepare for it by finding a quiet place where you can meet with God to talk or sing to him aloud.

The book of Psalms is a prayer book, and we can pray the psalms many ways. Today we'll pray them three ways: word for word, meditatively, and personalized.

Psalm 1

We've studied Psalm 1. Now that we know it well, let's worship with it by praying it aloud. Praying a Torah psalm is similar to pledging agreement.

> • Open your Bible to Psalm 1. Prayerfully read the psalm aloud to God.

The Little Details
Enclosure

Enclosure is also called *inclusio*, *inclusion*, and *envelope*. Psalm 1 frames the entire psalm by using enclosure in the first and last lines. Some psalms frame the beginning with the halfway point, or the halfway point with the last line.

Sometimes related psalms placed next to each other are joined by enclosure: Psalm 1's first line is linked to Psalm 2's last line with enclosure. That tells us those who arranged the Psalter considered the two psalms linked.

- - - - - - - - - - - - - - - - -

Now here's the irony: When we worship God with the psalms, the psalms transform our minds.

- - - - - - - - - - - - - - - - -

- Consider whether you hesitated when reading any part of the psalm. Did its message stir your full agreement, or did any part bring conviction? If conviction, pray for the Holy Spirit to bring your heart into alignment with God's words.
- *Optional:* Sing Psalm 1 to God.

Psalm 119

Psalm 119 is a Torah psalm that, like Psalm 1, celebrates the goodness of the Torah, God's instructions. It's also a **lament**, a petition for help in affliction. The affliction is twofold: an enemy's taunts and the psalmist's sorrow over not following God's instructions as well as he wishes. Through it, the psalmist is confident that God will not leave him, but will instead continue to teach and lead him.

We'll pray Psalm 119's first stanza verbatim first, and then we'll offer meditative prayer. Meditative prayer is talking to God about a Bible passage. We'll look for four things in the passage to talk to God about.

- Open your Bible to Psalm 119. Pray aloud the first stanza (verses 1-8).
- **Praise** God for something you see of his character in this passage.
- **Confess** anything that convicts you in the stanza.
- **Ask** for help to do something the stanza calls you to do.
- **Thank** God for something in the stanza.
- *Optional:* Continue reading as many of the psalm's remaining stanzas (through verse 176) as you have time to pray word for word and meditatively.

While working through this chapter, you've written a personalized psalm based on Psalm 1's message. Now you can offer it to God.

- Turn to the My Psalm page. Offer your psalm to God in prayer, and then read it aloud to him.
- Close by offering a prayer of thanksgiving for God's gracious care in telling us how to live a life that is blessed.

My Psalm

A Psalm of:

Praising

Confessing

Asking

Thanking

Creative Connection

I have always loved how God's Word is so visual and leads the reader to not only hear it, but to see its beauty as well. Some verses, of course, are more visual than others, and Psalm 1:3 is a perfect example. We can all visualize a tree, and we all know what leaves and fruit look like. So we have a good place to start. But sometimes as we take the time to meditate on a verse, God coaxes us to think outside the box—to "see" a little more than we did at first.

I love it every time I have an opportunity to share why my Psalm 1:3 illustration has been dubbed the "fruit cocktail" tree. In this psalm God says we will bear fruit, and what came to mind as I pondered verse 3 was that we, as believers in Christ, bear the fruit of the Spirit, which we know is multifaceted—love, peace, joy, and so much more. But we also bear the fruit of our labor in respect to using our gifts, talents, and abilities for God's glory. Because we are all created to be unique individuals, the fruit we bear through our good works will be as unique and varied as we are—hence, a "fruit cocktail" tree.

Also, where this verse says "in all that he does, he prospers," I thought about what God's perspective of prosperity might look like beyond financial gain or material blessing. The imagery of two birds and a nest came to mind. They symbolize the idea of our greatest prosperity being the spiritual heritage we pass down to our children, to our neighbors, and to so many others through the fruit we bear and the lives we live.

Be encouraged to take the time to meditate on God's Word and allow him time to stir your heart and open your spiritual eyes to create outside the box.

◉ Discover more creative inspiration.

Karla

Blessed is the one who delights in the word of God and meditates on it day and night... she will be like a Tree planted by streams of water, never withering, forever fruitful in season prospering always.

~ from Psalm 1 ~

©Karla Dornacher

Chapter 2

Psalm 2:
The Hope of Messiah's Reign

What is our hope when we suffer at the hands of wrongdoers?

Day 1

Introducing Psalm 2

In the last chapter we saw that Psalm 1 tells us the righteous delight in God's instructions but the wicked mock them. While that gives us hope in how to live the blessed life, it produces a quandary: Those who want to live according to God's ways dwell among those who do not. Some people rebel against the laws God gives to protect and bless us, and their rebellion causes suffering.

Our newspapers display the evidence daily. Terrorists murder and maim. Con artists bilk the elderly. The rich exploit the poor. Abusers scar children. Liars lock the innocent behind bars.

Each of us has our own stories of wrongs perpetrated against us and our loved ones. And we know in our hearts we've hurt others.

What is our hope when we suffer wrongfully? The psalm we will look at today tells us.

It's a psalm originally composed for singing at the coronations of kings descended from David. It's one of about ten psalms categorized as **royal psalms** because they're about the Davidic monarchy.

A good, effective king was a cause for rejoicing, as 2 Chronicles 9:8 explains:

> Blessed be the LORD your God, who has delighted in you and set you on his throne as king for the LORD your God! Because your God loved Israel and would establish them forever, he has made you king over them, that you may execute justice and righteousness.

Such a king fought wickedness, judged righteously, executed justice, defended the poor, and crushed oppressors. A godly king brought the hope of justice and righteousness to the kingdom.

As for me I have set MY KING on ZION my holy hill

Psalm 2:6

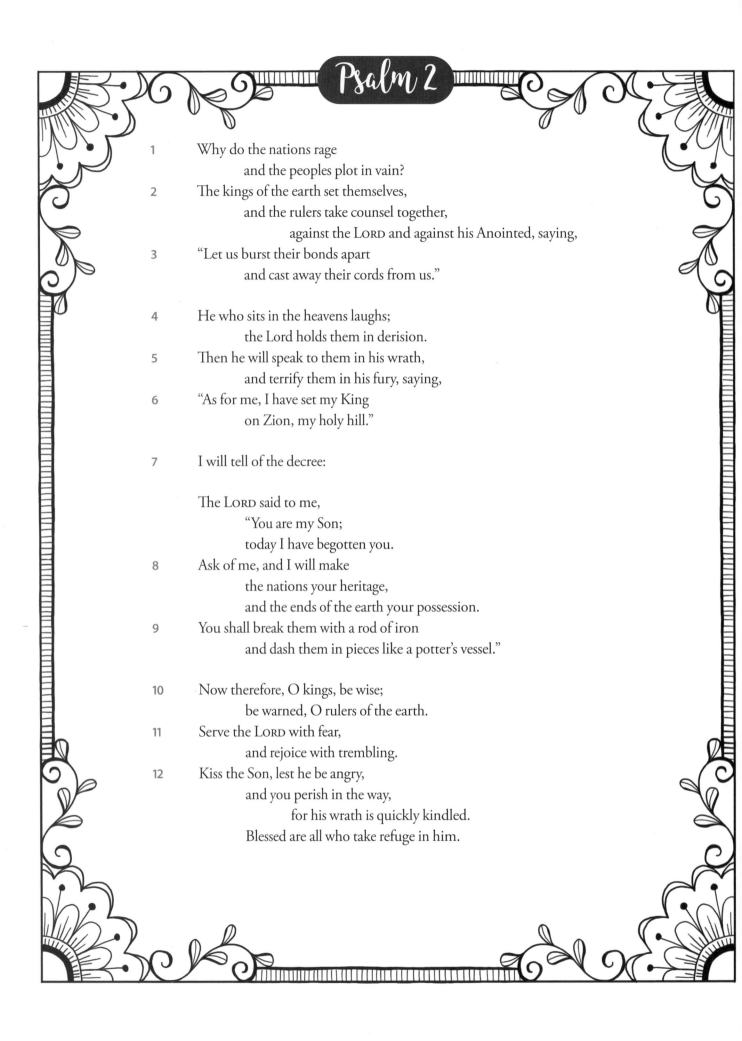

1   Why do the nations rage
         and the peoples plot in vain?

2   The kings of the earth set themselves,
         and the rulers take counsel together,
             against the Lord and against his Anointed, saying,

3   "Let us burst their bonds apart
         and cast away their cords from us."

4   He who sits in the heavens laughs;
         the Lord holds them in derision.

5   Then he will speak to them in his wrath,
         and terrify them in his fury, saying,

6   "As for me, I have set my King
         on Zion, my holy hill."

7   I will tell of the decree:

     The Lord said to me,
         "You are my Son;
         today I have begotten you.

8   Ask of me, and I will make
         the nations your heritage,
         and the ends of the earth your possession.

9   You shall break them with a rod of iron
         and dash them in pieces like a potter's vessel."

10   Now therefore, O kings, be wise;
         be warned, O rulers of the earth.

11   Serve the Lord with fear,
         and rejoice with trembling.

12   Kiss the Son, lest he be angry,
         and you perish in the way,
             for his wrath is quickly kindled.
         Blessed are all who take refuge in him.

A *type* is a person or thing that foreshadows something greater to come. Since ancient Israel was a type of the heavenly kingdom, and King David was a type of King Jesus, royal psalms often have elements that apply to the kingdom of heaven and to Jesus' reign. This psalm is no exception, and the New Testament quotes it frequently, applying its words to Jesus, the Son of David. Since it foretells the crowning of Jesus the Anointed One—Messiah—it is also a **messianic psalm**.

In the lessons ahead, we'll see how this psalm applied to David's sons, who ruled long ago, as well as to God's Son, whose kingdom comes. Understanding its original context will help us understand its messianic context.

For now, pray that God will speak to you through his words. Read the psalm.[1] As you read, don't worry if some parts don't fully make sense yet—this psalm requires a little knowledge of Jewish customs and we'll cover all that later.

> 1. ◗ What stands out to you most from your initial reading of this psalm?

The Big Picture

Psalm 2 has no inscription with an author's name, but Peter and John identify David as its author in Acts 4:25.

As with many psalms, the psalm's center line tells us its focus.

> 2. (a) In Psalm 2:7a, of what will the speaker tell? (b) Who spoke the decree (7b)?

Psalm 2 is about a decree God made about King David. When David wanted to build a temple for the Lord, he asked the prophet Nathan to ask God if that would be acceptable.

That night the Lord spoke to Nathan and told him to tell David no, David would not build a house (that is, a temple) for God, but rather God would build a house (that is, a dynasty) for David.

> 3. Read 2 Samuel 7:12-16. (a) What did Nathan tell David God would raise up for him (verse 12)? (b) What would this person do (verse 13)? (c) What would the Lord do for this person (verse 13)? (d) With what words does the Lord describe his relationship with that person (verse 14)? (e) What did the Lord promise David (verse 16)?

The Little Details
The Royal Psalms

2	King's coronation
18	King's battle victory
20	Prayer for king for battle victory
21	Praise by king for battle victory
45	King's wedding
72	Prayer for king's dominion
89	Davidic covenant
101	King's charter
110	Priestly kingdom
144	Peace by king's victory

Some Bible translations capitalize the words *anointed*, *king*, and *son* in Psalm 2 to make sure we don't miss their connection to Jesus. Others don't capitalize because doing so can cause readers to miss the psalm's original use, and because the original Hebrew didn't have upper- and lowercase letters.

This decree declared to David that his throne would be established forever. It was thus the authority by which all the sons of David ruled.

God later told David that he had chosen one of his sons to rule after him and to build the temple.

> 4. (a) Which of David's sons did God choose to reign after David (1 Chronicles 28:5)? (b) How did God describe the relationship he would have with David's son (verse 6)? (c) What was the condition for establishing this son's kingdom forever (verse 7)?

Solomon was not David's oldest living son, but David obeyed God's word despite the family turmoil doing so would cause. Before he died, he made Solomon king, probably presenting this psalm to him for his coronation.

But Solomon only partially fulfilled God's promise to David. David's descendants did not remain true to God, and their reign continued for only four centuries after David's death. A thousand years after David, another of his descendants came to finally fulfill the promise: Jesus. He will be the One who will reign forever and end evil.

You see, the rebellious rulers in Psalm 2:1 are not just human rulers. Long ago God created the earth and gave Adam and Eve reign over it. But an angel in the heavenly realms rebelled. In the guise of a serpent, he deceived Eve into believing God's plans for her and Adam were bad for them. As a result, she disobeyed God's command that forbade eating fruit from the Tree of the Knowledge of Good and Evil.

Too late, Eve realized her error. God in his grace promised her a child who would one day crush the serpent's head. But ever since, her descendants have tasted of good and evil on earth.

Meanwhile, the rebellious angel—Satan—continued to deceive as the prince of the power of the air and the ruler of the world.[2]

But Satan's rebellion will not last forever, for the One promised to Eve is the One promised to David. At the end of the age, this world and all its desires will pass away (1 John 2:16-17). Satan will be thrown into the lake of fire. The dead will rise, and those who have refused to submit to God's rule will be judged and will likewise be thrown into the lake of fire, an event called the second death (Revelation 20:10-15).

Then there will be a new heaven and a new earth, and those whose names are written in the Book of Life will dwell there with God and with the Lamb of God, Jesus.

> 5. Read Revelation 21:3-4. What stands out to you most about the new heaven and earth? Why?

Satan's rebellion will not last forever, for the One promised to Eve is the One promised to David.

6. Read Revelation 21:27. What will be absent?

Imagine no more evil, no more temptation, no more deception, no more dark spiritual forces vying for our souls. Imagine being with God. Imagine no more death nor mourning nor crying nor pain.

7. What do you long for most about the new heaven and earth? Why?

Experiencing Psalm 2 Creatively

Begin thinking of other ways to interact with Psalm 2. For inspiration, look back at Chapter 1, Day 1. Here are some ideas specific to Psalm 2:

- Use color and art in a way that encourages God's promises to speak to your heart (see this chapter's Creative Connection).

- Display a toy trumpet or an angel blowing a trumpet to remind you that King Jesus is coming and all that is wrong will be made right.

- If you're struggling with envy, pray daily for God's blessings on those you've envied. Ask God to show you his will for your life and to give you strength to submit to it.

The Little Details
Fun Facts for Poetry Lovers

In the last chapter we talked about poetic lines containing parallel segments, and about poetic lines being grouped in stanzas. If you read scholarly works, the terms are different. A *line segment* is usually called a *colon* (plural *cola*), although Hebrew scholar Robert Alter doesn't like the association with intestines and soft drinks and uses *verset*.[3]

The lines of Hebrew poems are usually said to be grouped into a **strophe** (rhymes with *trophy*), and groups of **strophes** (rhymes with *trophies*) on a similar theme form a stanza. For example, Psalm 139 has two stanzas: verses 1-18 are on the nature of God and verses 19-24 are on the elimination of evil; the first stanza has four strophes and the second has two.[4]

Because most readers are likely unfamiliar with the terms *colon* and *strophe*, I'll use *line segment* and *stanza* in this discovery book.

Hope Alive

If you're like me, you feel as though there is never enough time in your day! Have you ever had thoughts like, *Yeah, I want to spend time in Bible study, but...*

- *I am so busy.* (Yes, you are! But we all get the same 24 hours a day.)
- *I have to work.* (Have you asked God to help you create time in your day for him?)
- *I was never a great student in school.* (God is more powerful than your GPA.)
- *I want an easier way to grow with God.* (Remember Psalm 1? Those roots grow strong only when watered.)
- *I am just a regular woman, not some leader, speaker, or teacher.* (The more you get into God's Word, the more everyday people you will meet: fishermen, tax collectors, moms with kids, and shepherds who play vital roles in God's plan—just like you!)

Spending time in the Word will save you time because you'll gain the information to discern, and then stay on, God's best plan for your life. But to keep tracking with Christ, you'll need to set aside daily time with the Creator. God is the maker of time, so he has a supernatural way of s...t...r...e...t...c...h...i...n...g the minutes in your day. Here is why God can multiply your time:

- *God existed before "time" began:* "In the beginning God..." (Genesis 1:1).
- *God set time in motion:* "God said, 'Let there be light'...And God separated the light from the darkness. God called the light Day" (Genesis 1:3-5).
- *God is the exalted King:* He sees all from his throne, so he knows what is truly important in life. "God reigns over nations; God sits on his holy throne" (Psalm 47:8).
- *God orders our steps:* "The steps of a good man are ordered by the LORD" (Psalm 37:23 KJV); "In their hearts humans plan their course, but the LORD determines their steps" (Proverbs 16:9 NIV).

When I was 19, my mentor asked me, "How's your daily quiet time with God?" I thought I was too busy to fit in time with God, so I laid out a few of those standard excuses. My mentor countered with a piercing question: "Are you telling me you're too busy to spend time daily with the God who created you and created every second of your day, and loved you so much he spent his divine time to walk the steps up Golgotha's hill to be nailed on a cross and lay down his life for you?" *(Gulp.)*

As I pondered how to answer this question, I felt it was really God who was asking it. I was confronted with a "watershed moment," that pivot point when you know the choice you make will send you on a life-impacting trajectory with long-term consequences. This is the same question posed to us in Psalm 2: "Who is on the throne of your life? Whom do you call King?"

Make a decision today to keep Jesus as the King of Kings.

⏺ Download and complete the Quiet Time Commitment form to gain light by daily following the One who calls himself the Light of the world.

Pam

Day 2

The People Conspire

Whether for birthdays, new years, graduations, or weddings, we enjoy celebrating in song the milestones that mark the start of something new. Songs express the hope we have for a happy future, even though we know there will be challenges.

Coronations in ancient Israel were no different, and songs such as Psalm 2 were part of those great celebrations. So that we can understand Psalm 2 better, we'll look at what this psalm meant to the sons of David at their coronations, and then at what it means when applied to Jesus.

The Sons of David

Coronations were festive, but they also brought challenges. In those days, the start of a new reign by an inexperienced king was the prime time to revolt. Subject kings (called *vassals*) might rebel. So might unhappy Israelite tribes.

When the time drew near for David to pass the throne to Solomon, the revolt came from David's household. Adonijah, David's oldest living son, conspired with the army's commander and the high priest to take the throne for himself while David lay sick in bed (1 Kings 1). The conspiracy was treasonous and surely involved plans to kill Solomon, who would be a threat to Adonijah's throne when word got out that Solomon had been David's choice.

8. Read the psalm's first stanza (Psalm 2:1-3). (a) How does it fit Solomon's situation? (b) God had chosen Solomon to be the next king; why then was the "plot in vain" (verse 1)?

Perhaps Adonijah didn't believe God had chosen Solomon, or perhaps he just thought God was unfair. Either way, he conspired to circumvent God's plan.

9. According to Psalm 2:2, against whom are the rulers rebelling?

The prophet Nathan discovered Adonijah's plot and informed David of it. David was bedridden, but his mind was sharp. He responded swiftly and rushed Nathan and the priest Zadok to anoint Solomon king.

When God chose a king who was not next in line of succession, he sent a prophet to anoint him king with oil. When the successor was a son of the prior king, a priest anointed him king.[5] Both the prophet Nathan and the priest Zadok anointed Solomon (1 Kings 1:45), showing that both God and David chose him.

The Little Details

What Happened to the Kings?

As centuries passed, the Jewish kings and people abandoned their commitment to God. They worshiped other gods. The rich oppressed the poor and needy. Violence ran rampant. The courts were corrupt. Godly people cried, "Why, God, aren't you stopping this?" (see Habakkuk 1:1-4).

God sent prophets to call the people to repent lest he remove them as a nation, as Moses had warned would happen. They refused to listen. Finally, in 586 BC, Babylon conquered the nation, smashed Jerusalem's walls, burned the temple, and exiled the people.

But the prophets had coupled their messages of impending doom with messages of future hope. The exile would be temporary, and one day an anointed king descended from David again would rule. He would fulfill God's promise to David.

A newly anointed and crowned king was called *the Lord's anointed*.

A newly anointed and crowned king was called *the Lord's anointed*.

> **10.** Why was rebellion against the Lord's anointed king equal to rebellion against the Lord (Psalm 2:2)?

The next verse refers to *bonds* and *cords*. The Israelites used these to attach the yoke of a cart or plow to an animal's neck so it could serve them.

> **11.** (a) What do the rebels want to do (Psalm 2:3)? (b) They considered themselves to be like an ox tied to a yoke and forced to serve its master. What are some reasons people rebel against a godly king whose goal is to rule righteously?

We've seen how the first stanza spoke to people in the days of the sons of David who became kings, and in particular to Solomon. Before continuing to the next stanza, let's look at how it applies to a later Son: Jesus.

The Son of God

Jump ahead almost a thousand years. Israel no longer exists as a nation. Instead, Jews live in a few Roman districts. The Jews have no king (see the "What Happened to the Kings?" sidebar), but based on God's decree to David, they eagerly await the arrival of a son of David to rule.

In Psalm 2:2, the word translated *anointed* is the Hebrew word from which we get our English word *messiah*. Psalm 2 gave the Jews hope in Messiah's reign.

They had Isaiah's writings that said the Lord God would anoint this Messiah, causing the Spirit of the Lord to be on him (Isaiah 61:1). The prophet John the Baptist describes seeing this happen.

> **12.** (a) In Mark 1:10, whom did John see descend upon Jesus? (b) What did he hear the Lord say from heaven (Mark 1:11)?

Acts 10:38 tells us this began Jesus' ministry:

> God anointed Jesus of Nazareth with the Holy Spirit and with power. He went about doing good and healing all who were oppressed by the devil, for God was with him.

Jesus preached with authority, healed the sick, and cast out demons. Through miracles he showed he was the Messiah about whom the prophets spoke.

But Jesus wasn't the type of messiah everyone wanted. Most wanted a warrior to break them free from foreign rule and establish his kingdom on earth, as in the days of David. The Jewish spiritual leaders wanted a warrior submissive to them.

God had a much bigger plan. Yes, Jesus was Messiah. But he spoke of the kingdom of heaven and said his kingdom wasn't of this world (John 18:36).

The Jewish leaders, envious over the crowds that followed Jesus, delivered him to Pilate to be crucified. Pilate could find no justification for crucifixion and sought to free him, but he failed. He crucified Jesus, putting this inscription of the charges against him over his head: "The King of the Jews" (Mark 15:26).

13. Read Peter and John's prayer in Acts 4:24-27, which quotes Psalm 2:1-2. (a) Whom did they say spoke through David when he wrote Psalm 2 (verse 25)? (b) Whom did they say the people had raged and plotted against (verse 27)? (c) What rulers and peoples conspired against Jesus?

As Adonijah had conspired against Solomon, so the Jewish leaders conspired against Jesus.

14. ☾ Adonijah and the chief priests were driven by envy. (a) What can we learn from these two stories about times when God seems to advance someone else in a position we hoped to have ourselves? (b) What are ways you deal righteously with disappointment and envy?

The Jewish and Roman leaders weren't the only rulers conspiring against Jesus. Revelation 12 symbolizes what was happening in the heavenly realms. Satan, the ruler of this world,[6] is depicted as a great, red dragon who tries to devour the child born "to rule all the nations with a rod of iron" (Revelation 12:5). But the child is caught up to God and his throne, and Satan is hurled to the earth.

15. ♪ For this chapter we'll write a psalm about the kingdom of God. On the My Psalm page at the end of this chapter, write your name to the right of the heading, "A Psalm of," and then write a prayer telling God about the things you long for most in the kingdom to come.

The Little Details

Anthropomorphisms

"Sits," "laughs," and "holds them in derision" in Psalm 2 are all *anthropomorphisms*: figures of speech that compare God with a human trait to communicate a truth about him in a way we can understand. God doesn't literally sit, but human kings sit on thrones to rule, and so we understand God sitting in heaven to mean he rules from heaven. Although God does have passions and emotions, he doesn't literally laugh or deride, but these terms show us how foolish the rebels' conspiracies are to the all-powerful God, who knows the future.[7]

Zion

David captured the stronghold of Zion, renamed it City of David, and enlarged it (2 Samuel 5:7-9). It was on a ridge along the southeastern edge of Jerusalem. The name *Zion* later came to refer to the temple site, and even later to all of Jerusalem.

Day 3

The Lord and the King Speak

Sometimes people look at all the troubles in the world and think God can't be in control. Psalm 2 paints a different picture, a picture of God seeing rebellion and declaring it futile because its end is coming.

The Lord Speaks

Let's again begin with the conspiracy against Solomon.

The Sons of David

Although God had chosen Solomon to be king and build his temple, Adonijah conspired to seize the crown for himself.

> **16.** Read Psalm 2:4-9. How does the Lord react to plotting and turbulence among people who conspire against his plans (verse 4)?

> **17.** ♩ (a) Why do you think God isn't worried about what humans plan against him or those he's anointed? (b) How does this comfort you?

The word translated *Lord* is a title designating a master/servant relationship. Its use shows the conspirators owe obedience to the One enthroned in heaven.

> **18.** (a) According to Psalm 2:5, how would God treat those who come against his anointed king? (b) Why should hearing that God is against them terrify the rebels?

Unaware that prophet and priest had anointed Solomon king, Adonijah feasted and celebrated what he thought was his success.

The Son of God

Just as Adonijah plotted against Solomon and thought he'd succeeded, so also those who crucified Jesus thought they'd succeeded. But their plans were in vain, for God did something they never imagined. Ephesians 1:20-21 tells us what:

He raised him from the dead and seated him at his right hand in the heavenly places, far above all rule and authority and power and dominion, and above every name that is named, not only in this age but also in the one to come.

The Jewish leaders may have celebrated their victory over Jesus, but they were unaware that God had indeed set his King on Zion as he proclaimed in Psalm 2:6—not the earthly Zion within Jerusalem, but the heavenly Mount Zion in the heavenly Jerusalem, the city of the living God.[8]

Just as Adonijah continued to feast unaware that Solomon had taken dominion, so now many live in rebellion against God, unaware that Jesus has taken dominion.

19. ♪ How does God's power to bring about what he promises make you feel?

20. 🎵 On the My Psalm page, leave a blank line to indicate a new stanza, and then write a prayer telling God how his power to bring about what he decrees gives you hope.

The King Speaks

In Psalm 2's next stanza, the new king speaks.

The Sons of David

As the holy oil dripped on Solomon's head, he must have thought about God's promises to David while memories of the moment he heard God had chosen him—yes, him!—to rule next and to build God's temple swept through his mind.

21. In Psalm 2:7a, of what does the newly anointed king tell?

God's decree about him is his authority to rule.

22. What did the Lord say to the king (Psalm 2:7c-d)?

God told David he would be a father to David's son (2 Samuel 7:14). He promised to have a special relationship with him: just as a father is to a son, so would God be to the king. On the day a Davidic king was crowned, he became God's son in this special way and inherited the kingdom from God.

As the holy oil dripped on Solomon's head, he must have thought about God's promises to David.

The Little Details
Potter's Vessel

The second line in Psalm 2:9 may refer to an Egyptian custom. A Pharaoh wrote the name of each city in his domain on a votive jar and placed it in the temple. If a city rebelled, he dashed the jar to pieces in the temple, terrifying the people.[9]

23. What did the Lord say the king could ask of him (Psalm 2:8)?

Solomon would eventually extend the kingdom's borders to the full extent promised to Abraham.

24. (a) What authority and power does God give the anointed king (Psalm 2:9)? (b) How does this explain the futility of the rebels' plans (verse 1)?

Solomon felt the golden crown descend upon his head and rest there. He now had the authority, power, and responsibility to rule justly, protect the people God had just given him, and crush rebellion. Most of the kingdom didn't know that, though, for the trumpets had not yet sounded.

The Son of God

Jump ahead again to the King crowned on the heavenly Mount Zion. In Acts 13:32-33, the apostle Paul told the Jews Jesus had fulfilled the promise in Psalm 2:

> And we bring you the good news that what God promised to the fathers, this he has fulfilled to us their children by raising Jesus, as also it is written in the second Psalm, "You are my Son, today I have begotten you."

We saw that God called the kings descended from David "sons." But the relationship between the Davidic kings and the Lord God merely foreshadowed the greater, unique relationship between Jesus and his Father.

25. Read Luke 1:32-35. (a) According to the angel Gabriel's words to Mary, why was Jesus called the Son of God? (b) What throne would God give him (verse 32)? (c) How long will he reign and how long will his kingdom last (verse 33)?

The angel called David Jesus' father because David was Jesus' ancestor through both his mother, Mary, and his adopted father, Joseph (Matthew 1:1). But Jesus was also the only begotten Son of God, conceived not from an earthly father but by the Holy Spirit.

26. 🎵 On the My Psalm page, skip a line to indicate a new stanza, and then write a prayer about what impresses you most about Jesus' righteous rule and the way he paid sin's penalty to bring us into his kingdom. Ask for his kingdom to come.

In Psalm 2:8, God offers the Messiah the nations and the ends of the earth. Isaiah 49:6 tells us God's words to the Messiah:

> It is too light a thing that you should be my servant to raise up the tribes of Jacob and to bring back the preserved of Israel; I will make you as a light for the nations, that my salvation may reach to the end of the earth.

He was anointed to rule not just Jews—the "tribes of Jacob"—but people from all nations. Ever since Jesus ascended to heaven, his followers have spread the word about God's kingdom to people throughout the earth.

The Psalm Warns

The king is crowned, and now the psalm addresses the rebels.

The Sons of David

Back at Solomon's coronation, the trumpets blew and the people erupted in praise and thanksgiving to God for having chosen a king to rule and to bring peace and justice.

But not everyone celebrated.

Down in the valley, Adonijah and his guests heard the uproar and felt the ground shake. They wondered what it meant and hoped for good tidings. But then someone brought terrifying news: Solomon had been crowned king.

The guests fled. Adonijah begged Solomon for his life.

Solomon could have executed Adonijah for treason. Instead, he offered a warning similar to that in Psalm 2's last stanza.

> **27.** Read Psalm 2's last stanza (verses 10-12). (a) What two things does Psalm 2:10 tell the rebels to do? (b) This verse is a chiasm with "be wise" parallel to "be warned." Why are these two instructions to rebels equivalent? (c) How does this warning show grace and patience?

> **28.** (a) Whom should all in the kingdom serve (Psalm 2:11)? (b) Why is submitting to the ruler the Lord puts in place equated with serving the Lord? (c) Why should fear of the consequences of rebellion guide them?

In the ancient Near East, kissing a ruler signified submission and homage.

> **29.** In Psalm 2:12, what would happen to those who refuse to kiss the new king? (The one who is angry could be either the newly anointed king or God, who has already expressed his anger in verse 5.)

Three bits of advice: Wisely take warning; serve the Lord God; submit to his chosen king. To ignore the advice is to perish.

Solomon showed Adonijah this grace in similar words: "If he will show himself a worthy man, not one of his hairs shall fall to the earth, but if wickedness is found in him, he shall die" (1 Kings 1:52).

Adonijah bowed before King Solomon and lived.

David arranged for a second coronation for Solomon, more elaborate than the first hasty one when David lay ill. He stood before the crowd and told how God had chosen Solomon to be king and build a temple. The people celebrated with worship, thousands of sacrifices, and joyful feasting (1 Chronicles 29:22).

Although Adonijah's knee bowed, his heart did not. After David died, he made another play for the throne. Solomon executed Adonijah and the army commander, and he banished the former high priest (1 Kings 2:13-25).

Solomon's rule was then firmly in place.

> **30.** Who is blessed, according to Psalm 2:12d?

Indeed, 1 Kings 4:24-25 says those who sought refuge in Solomon were blessed:

> [Solomon] had dominion over all the region west of the Euphrates from Tiphsah to Gaza, over all the kings west of the Euphrates. And he had peace on all sides around him. And Judah and Israel lived in safety, from Dan even to Beersheba, every man under his vine and under his fig tree, all the days of Solomon.

Solomon, whose name means "man of peace,"[10] reigned 40 years and built an earthly temple of earth's stones for God's name. His reign brought peace to the kingdom of Israel.

Solomon was a type of the Prince of Peace who reigns forever and who now is building a spiritual temple of living stones—the people of God. His reign brings peace with God to the kingdom of heaven.[11]

The Son of God

And now we return to this Prince of Peace.

When Jesus ascended to heaven, his disciples proclaimed that Jesus was the Messiah and had sat down at the Father's right hand. They offered grace: Be wise and warned, serve the Lord God, and submit to his Son Jesus as ruler so that you will not perish, but have eternal life. Today Christians continue to spread this message.

For one day, trumpets will sound.

> **31.** What will happen when Jesus sends his angels out with a trumpet call (Matthew 24:31)?

The Little Details
New High Priest

At Solomon's second coronation, Zadok was anointed as the new high priest (1 Chronicles 29:22). A concurrent anointing of king and high priest is another way Solomon's coronation is a type of Jesus' coronation, for on his ascension Jesus became both king and high priest (Hebrews 5:5-6).

- - - - - - - - - - - - - - - - -

Solomon was a type of the Prince of Peace who reigns forever and who now is building a spiritual temple of living stones—the people of God.

- - - - - - - - - - - - - - - - -

32. Read Matthew 13:24-30 and 36-43. (a) What will Jesus send his angels to gather out of his kingdom (verse 41)? (b) What will happen to them (verse 42)? (c) What will happen to the children of the kingdom (verse 43)?

33. Read Revelation 22:3-5. (a) What will be missing from this kingdom (verse 3)? (b) Who will be there (verses 3-4)? (c) What will the Lord's servants do (verses 3-5)?

Jesus will take into his kingdom those who belong to him and will judge those who do not. At that judgment, those who've ignored the warning to serve the Lord will face God's wrath and perish in the second death, the lake of fire.[12] Everything that causes sin will be consumed.

But those who take refuge in the Son will dwell in the new heaven and new earth, finally and forever safe from the wickedness that infects this world. There they will reign with Christ forever.

What the Israelite kings achieved imperfectly, King Jesus completes perfectly.

That is our hope. One day God through Jesus will judge angels and humans, and he will end evil.

34. What impresses you most about the grace King Jesus offers?

35. On the My Psalm page at the end of this chapter, skip a line to indicate a new stanza, and then write a prayer submitting yourself to Jesus as your King and asking for others to do likewise.

Day 5

The Beginning and the End

Today we'll begin by looking at how Psalms 1 and 2 serve as the introduction to the book of Psalms. Then we'll look more closely at what it means to worship with royal psalms.

The Psalter's Introduction: Psalms 1 and 2

What is it about Psalms 1 and 2 that cause scholars to view them as an introductory unit? Psalm 1's description of the ideal man and Psalm 2's portrait of the ideal king play a part. But also important is the fact that the last line of Psalm 2 links back to the first line of Psalm 1, forming enclosure. Let's take a look at how the two psalms relate.

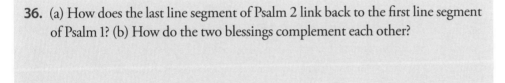

36. (a) How does the last line segment of Psalm 2 link back to the first line segment of Psalm 1? (b) How do the two blessings complement each other?

37. (a) The word translated *meditate* in Psalm 1:2 is the same word translated *plot* in Psalm 2:1. Contrast what the godly meditate on in Psalm 1:2 with what those in Psalm 2:1-3 meditate on. (b) Contrast the motives behind the meditations.

38. Compare who perishes in Psalm 1:6 with who perishes in Psalm 2:12.

39. How do Psalm 1's encouragement to know and obey God's will and Psalm 2's encouragement to serve the Messiah complement each other?

Psalm 1 speaks of the righteous man, and Psalm 2 of the king who saves him. Together they tell us that the way of blessing is to live as a righteous person submitted to God's chosen King.

Our Lord, Come!

"Maranatha!" There in one word is the cry, "Our Lord, come!" (1 Corinthians 16:22). It encapsulates what Jesus teaches us to pray: "Your kingdom come, your will be done, on earth as it is in heaven" (Matthew 6:10).

When we pray for God's kingdom to come, we express our yearning for that kingdom, where our Lord rules with righteousness and justice. We offer ourselves as obedient servants longing to dwell under his reign. We agree that God's commands are right and holy, and that justice demands sin's wages paid. We give thanks for Jesus paying the penalty for our sins through his death on the cross so that we might live. We trust that as he rose from the dead, so shall we.

Our English word *worship* comes from the Old English *weorthscipe*, which meant "to ascribe worth, to pay homage, to reverence or to venerate."[13] Praying "Our Lord, come!" declares the Lord's worthiness to rule and our willingness to be ruled.

The biblical concept of worship is broader. The word translated *worship* in the Old Testament means "bow oneself down low to the ground." Likewise, one of the words translated *worship* in the New Testament also means to bow down or kneel. Another means to give reverential homage.[14]

Old Testament professor Allen P. Ross describes the words like this:

> Thus both Testaments use words for bowing down and giving homage to mean worship in general. To bow down before someone, a king or God, is to show adoration, devotion, submission, and service; and by the physical act of bowing the object of the veneration appears higher and so is exalted.[15]

Bowing shows submission and is an act of worship in itself. Worshiping with bodies, minds, and spirits engages us completely. Bowing shows humble submission, adoring devotion, and aching anticipation of Jesus' reign in the new heaven and new earth. Paul explains in Philippians 2:9-11:

> God has highly exalted him and bestowed on him the name that is above every name, so that at the name of Jesus every knee should bow, in heaven and on earth and under the earth, and every tongue confess that Jesus Christ is Lord, to the glory of God the Father.

On judgment day, some will bow as the conquered bow, yielding to the inevitable with trembling. But those who willingly bowed on earth will bow then in gladness and joy, the hope of Jesus' reign finally come.

Maranatha!

Worshiping with Royal Psalms

Find a quiet place where you can bow down or kneel as you worship with psalms that express your longing for Jesus' reign in heaven. If your health doesn't permit bowing or kneeling on the floor, bend from the waist or bow your head; what we *can* give counts, not what we cannot.

When we pray for God's kingdom to come, we express our yearning for that kingdom, where our Lord rules with righteousness and justice.

Psalm 2

We'll begin by praying Psalm 2 word for word and meditatively.

- Open your Bible to Psalm 2. In a prayerful attitude, read the psalm aloud slowly. Pause between lines to let their full meaning sink into your heart.

- Pray meditatively over Psalm 2: **Praise** God for what you see of his character; **confess** anything you're convicted about; **ask** for God's help in serving him and in telling others about him; and **thank** him that his kingdom comes.

- *Optional:* Sing Psalm 2 to the Lord.

Psalm 101

In Psalm 101, David pledges to reign righteously. This psalm may have been sung at coronations along with Psalm 2.

- Read Psalm 101 slowly, meditating on what it meant to David and the Israelites who heard him make this pledge. Note that "house" (verses 2,7) refers to the administrative house; those who "minister to" him (verse 6) are the royal staff; and one of the king's duties (verse 8) was to hear court cases.

- Read Psalm 101 again aloud, meditating on what it would mean for you to pledge these words in one of your areas of leadership, such as parenting, work, or service.

- Read Psalm 101 a third time, this time meditating on what it will be like to dwell with King Jesus, who alone will perfectly fulfill this pledge.

- Pray meditatively over Psalm 101: **Praise** God for what you see of his character; **confess** anything that you're convicted about; **ask** for help to do what Psalm 101 calls you to do; and **thank** God for its message.

My Psalm

Finish by worshiping with the psalm you wrote.

- Turn to the My Psalm page. Offer the psalm to God in prayer, and then read your psalm aloud to him.

- Close by praying for the Lord's return and offering thanks for the blessing bestowed on all who take refuge in King Jesus.

Bowing shows humble submission, adoring devotion, and aching anticipation of Jesus' reign in the new heaven and new earth.

My Psalm ——————————————————————

A Psalm of:

Creative Connection

I can still remember, as a child, sitting for hours with my coloring book and a rainbow assortment of crayons beckoning me to carefully outline and fill the spaces. I loved to draw even then, but the only coloring I recall was reserved for the pages of these treasured books. Maybe that's why I draw and offer free coloring pages for kids on my website and have for years, partly knowing children today enjoy this quiet pastime as much as I did. But even more importantly I want children to focus not just on the art of coloring but on the truth of God's Word. And that's my heart's desire for you as well.

Coloring can be restful and relaxing. For some it's also therapeutic and stress-reducing. For others it's simply an avenue for creative fun. But the truth is, when you combine the simple creative act of coloring with the power of being in God's Word, there is the potential to change one's thoughts and even one's life. So please, as you color the illustrations in this discovery book, take the time to slowly read the verses, meditating on each phrase. Memorize them. And allow his truths and his promises to speak to your heart and settle down into your spirit.

With this chapter's illustration consider choosing colors that reflect the royalty of the King of Kings—purples and reds and golds. And as you color the verse and the crown, declare the Lordship of Christ over your life and proclaim that he is seated on the throne of your heart. Take some time while you color to pray and ask God to show you any areas of your life where you might be rebelling against his rule, and then surrender your will to him anew.

👁 Discover more colored pencil techniques.

Karla

As for me, I have set MY KING on ZION, my holy hill

Psalm 2:6

Chapter 3

Psalm 51:
The Hope of Mercy

What would God have us do when we've sinned?

Day 1

Introducing Psalm 51

At 19, I worked for a tiny family photography studio in a dusty strip mall. The photographer owner had only one other employee, an Italian woman with long, dark curls; thick eyeliner; and fire-truck-red lipstick and nails. Irene came from New York and said "grammar" instead of "grandma" and "gramma" instead of "grammar."

Despite a decade's difference in age, we became good friends. I told her I was a Christian, and she told me she used to be Catholic but didn't go to church anymore. Since I carried my burgundy faux leather Bible to work to read on breaks, if she remarked on a subject for which I knew a related Scripture, I'd read it to her. She liked that and was always surprised that the Bible said so much about regular life. I invited her to church, but she declined.

One afternoon Irene came to work with pale lips and her cheek looking like it was hiding an apple. She'd rushed over from having a root canal and had missed lunch. I offered to get her a milkshake, but she shooed me with her red manicured hand and said I'd worked my shift and should go home. Besides, neither of us knew any place nearby that sold milkshakes.

I walked out of the studio and surveyed the busy street just past the cracked asphalt parking lot. I prayed, "God, Irene really needs a milkshake. Could you show me where to find one?"

I approached a young man hurrying by to ask if he knew of a place, but he couldn't think of one either. I got in my pale blue Toyota Corona with the chipped hood and started driving, making clueless turns while praying. Suddenly, there in front of me, was a bright pink-and-blue Baskin Robbins sign. I parked, ran inside, and bought a chocolate milkshake.

Being directionally challenged, I prayed for help getting back to the studio and made it there quickly. When I walked in holding the frosty paper cup, Irene's eyes brimmed with tears. I explained how I'd found the shop and said, "God is showing you how much he loves you!"

Psalm 51

To the choirmaster. A Psalm of David, when Nathan the prophet went to him, after he had gone in to Bathsheba.

1 Have mercy on me, O God,
    according to your steadfast love;
according to your abundant mercy
    blot out my transgressions.
2 Wash me thoroughly from my iniquity,
    and cleanse me from my sin!

3 For I know my transgressions,
    and my sin is ever before me.
4 Against you, you only, have I sinned
    and done what is evil in your sight,
so that you may be justified in your words
    and blameless in your judgment.
5 Behold, I was brought forth in iniquity,
    and in sin did my mother conceive me.
6 Behold, you delight in truth in the inward being,
    and you teach me wisdom in the secret heart.

7 Purge me with hyssop, and I shall be clean;
    wash me, and I shall be whiter than snow.
8 Let me hear joy and gladness;
    let the bones that you have broken rejoice.
9 Hide your face from my sins,
    and blot out all my iniquities.

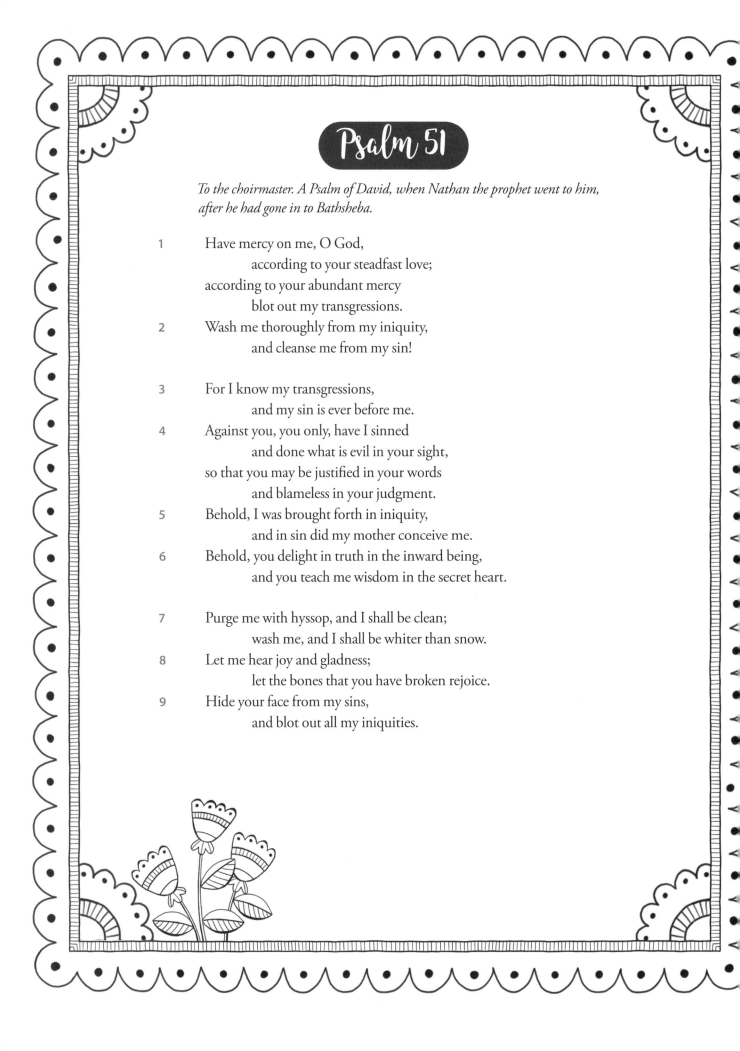

10 Create in me a clean heart, O God,
        and renew a right spirit within me.
11 Cast me not away from your presence,
        and take not your Holy Spirit from me.
12 Restore to me the joy of your salvation,
        and uphold me with a willing spirit.

13 Then I will teach transgressors your ways,
        and sinners will return to you.
14 Deliver me from bloodguiltiness, O God,
        O God of my salvation,
        and my tongue will sing aloud of your righteousness.
15 O Lord, open my lips,
        and my mouth will declare your praise.
16 For you will not delight in sacrifice, or I would give it;
        you will not be pleased with a burnt offering.
17 The sacrifices of God are a broken spirit;
        a broken and contrite heart, O God, you will not despise.

18 Do good to Zion in your good pleasure;
        build up the walls of Jerusalem;
19 then will you delight in right sacrifices,
        in burnt offerings and whole burnt offerings;
        then bulls will be offered on your altar.

The Little Details
Penitential Psalms

The early Christian church chose seven psalms for expressing repentance in church services. They help worshipers examine their lives and confess their sins.[1] These are the seven:[2]

6   A Prayer for Mercy

32   The Joy of Forgiveness

38   Prayer of a Suffering Sinner

51   A Prayer for Restoration

102   Affliction in Light of Eternity

130   Awaiting Redemption

143   A Cry for Help

The next day when we were alone she said quietly, "You've been trying so hard to make me a Christian and I need to tell you why I can't be one. I've never told anyone my terrible secret. Years ago when I met my husband, he was married to someone else. I had an affair with him. He divorced his wife and married me. So you see, God could never forgive me and I can never be a Christian."

Like Irene, many fear they've sinned so badly that God could never forgive them.

- A single woman ashamed over crossing sexual lines that she vowed never to cross can't stop saying, "I'm so bad; I'm so bad."
- A man ensnared in Internet porn keeps promising he'll never do it again. But after countless falls, he fears he's reached the limits of God's patience.
- A married woman looks at the ultrasound of her baby and suddenly wonders if that other baby, the one she was told was just "a clump of cells," looked like this. Her face burns crimson. Can God ever forgive her? She wants to ask someone, but is too afraid of their judgments. She suffers silently.

We handle our sin in different ways, from denial we've done wrong, to shoulder-shrugging complacency, to self-punishments, to paralyzing shame.

| Denial of Wrongdoing | Complacency | ??? | Self-Punishment | Paralyzing Shame |

What would God have us do when we've sinned?

Today's psalm will show us what King David did after he grievously sinned.

He'd led a mostly godly life up until then. People looked up to him as a righteous, trustworthy man. But in one afternoon, he betrayed that trust. To keep from being found out, he betrayed it even more.

Yet when God exposed his sin, he responded the way God wanted him to—and God forgave him.

He wrote this psalm in response to God laying bare his guilt. It's a psalm that dares to hope for mercy. It's one of seven **penitential psalms**.

Today we'll read Psalm 51 and look at the events leading up to its composition. If you, like Irene, think you could never belong to God because God could never forgive you, pray for God to open the eyes of your heart and read the psalm as a door to seeing his mercy. If you're a Christian, first ask God to search your heart and show you sins you haven't yet confessed, and then read the psalm.[3]

1. 🎵 What stands out to you from your initial reading of this psalm?

The Big Picture

2. According to the inscription at the top of the psalm, what occasioned its writing?

The prophet Nathan rebuked David over his secret affair with Bathsheba and the subsequent murder of her husband to cover up the affair when she became pregnant.

The problem started when King David was about 47.[4] One day he stayed behind in the palace while his army went off to war. He took a late afternoon stroll on his rooftop and spied a breathtakingly beautiful woman bathing. He asked around and discovered that she was the daughter of one of his best soldiers and the granddaughter of his most trusted advisor.

She was also the wife of Uriah, a member of David's special forces of 30 who were away at war.

David slept with her. Weeks later, she sent word she was pregnant.

David ordered her husband to the palace to bring him battle news. He told Uriah to spend the night with his wife. But Uriah didn't go home, so David arranged for him to die in battle. He brushed off his action, saying, "The sword devours now one and now another" (2 Samuel 11:25).

David married the grieving widow and she bore a son. It seemed he had gotten away with everything. But the Lord God had seen it all and sent the prophet Nathan to David.

3. Read 2 Samuel 12:1-6. (a) What did David say the rich man deserved (verse 5)? (b) What did David say the rich man had to do (verse 6)?

David followed the law, which required restoring a stolen sheep with four sheep (Exodus 22:1).

The Little Details
Staying Behind

Why did David stay behind at the palace?

The last four chapters of 2 Samuel are arranged topically, not chronologically. Chapter 21 describes an event that may tell us not only why David stayed behind, but why he was more susceptible to temptation: After David became weary in a battle and had to be rescued, his men told him he could not go with them to battle anymore (2 Samuel 21:17).

Dr. Robert D. Bergen, professor of Old Testament and biblical languages, says this event could have been prior to the affair with Bathsheba. He says David's staying behind "should not be understood as dereliction of duty," especially since he'd stayed behind before (2 Samuel 10:17).[5]

4. Read 2 Samuel 12:7-9. (a) Who was the rich man Nathan was talking about (verse 7)? (b) Why do you think God listed the immense blessings he had given David (verses 7-8)? (c) What had David despised (verse 9)? (d) In God's eyes, who killed Uriah (verse 9)?

The phrase, "I gave you…your master's wives," is talking about King Saul's wives. In the ancient Near East, when a king took another king's throne, he inherited the former king's wives and concubines and was responsible for their care.

5. Read 2 Samuel 12:10-12. (a) Who had David despised by taking Uriah's wife (verse 10)? (b) Was David going to escape judgment (verses 11-12)?

To lie with a king's wives was tantamount to claiming the king's throne!

6. Read 2 Samuel 12:13-14. (a) What was David's response (verse 13)? (b) The penalty for both adultery and murder was death. What mercy did the Lord show David (verse 13)? (c) Was he to escape consequences (verse 14)?

Later David wrote a prayer to God—a prayer we know now as Psalm 51. This prayer has six components we can use when we've sinned. The first is boldly asking God for mercy.

When my coworker Irene told me she couldn't become a Christian because she'd committed adultery, I asked her if she knew who King David was. She nodded. I said, "Did you know he committed both adultery and murder, and God forgave him?"

"What?" She leaned forward, her eyes and mouth wide open.

I told her the story of David and Bathsheba and how when a prophet rebuked David, David repented. I showed her verses about God's willingness to forgive. I asked, "If God forgave David for both adultery and murder, do you think he can forgive you?"

"Yes," she said quickly. "I may have committed adultery, but I'm not as bad as David. I sure never murdered anybody."

She gave her life to God right then. When she finished praying, she smiled broadly. The burden of guilt she'd carried for years was gone.

"If God forgave David for both adultery and murder, do you think he can forgive you?"

David's restoration brought Irene hope in God's mercy. My prayer is it will bring you, too, to place your hope in God's mercy.

Experiencing Psalm 51 Creatively

Begin thinking of other ways to interact with Psalm 51. For inspiration, review Chapter 1, Day 1 or visit www.DiscoveringHopeInThePsalms.com. Here are some ideas specific to this chapter's psalm:

- Use borders and symbols with Scripture to emphasize meaning (see this chapter's Creative Connection).

- Plant marjoram or thyme in a small container on which you've painted part of Psalm 51:7: "Purge me with hyssop, and I shall be clean."

- Label a basket with this part of Psalm 51:7: "Wash me and I shall be whiter than snow." Fill the basket with white towels and soap.

- Sketch one of the scenes from 2 Samuel 12:1-23.

Hope Alive

The home I grew up in loaded me with more baggage than you'd find in a 747! And God, through the power of his Word and promises, has unloaded that negative emotional baggage and replaced those heavy burdens with hope.

Hope arrives to rescue, redeem, restore, and renew us! It unburdens us so we can move on in God's purpose. This is what David came to understand in Psalm 51. I once drew a colorful, creative biblical expression of all the ways David begged God to free him from his sinful baggage: blot, wash, cleanse, justify, purge, hide, create, renew, restore, uphold, and so on. When David grasped that God rescues, a glimmer of hope became a resolve of obedience and dedication: "Then I will teach transgressors your ways, and sinners will return to you" (verse 13). In repentance and redemption, David gained traction to move forward in the calling God created for him to live out with conviction and godly pride.

Isaiah 64:8 explains, "We are the clay, and you are our potter; we are all the work of your hand." I see God's Word as the Potter's wheel because our lives are shaped and transformed on the foundation of Scripture. I have created a simple Bible study method to walk you through any passage and on to express the Word in an artistic form.

Take P.R.I.D.E. in Your Creative Biblical Expression

Reflect on these verses and take pride in anything you do for God, including how you study his Word and express the heart of it in an artistic way.

> In that day the Branch of the *Lord* will be beautiful and glorious, and the fruit of the land will be the pride and glory of the survivors in Israel (Isaiah 4:2 NIV, emphasis mine).

> If anyone speaks, they should do so as one who speaks the very words of God. If anyone serves, they should do so with the strength God provides, so that in all things God may be praised through Jesus Christ (1 Peter 4:11 NIV).

> And whatever you do, do it heartily, as to the Lord and not to men (Colossians 3:23).

Below are the simplified steps of the P.R.I.D.E. method:

*P*ray before beginning your Bible study with the goal of creative biblical expression. "Lord, let my artistic expressions be both biblical and beautiful to give glory to you. Amen."

*R*ead the entire chapter of the verse you selected. I like to write out the verses I'm working on so I slow down to see patterns, key words, or a word picture I may sense God calling me to draw.

*I*nvestigate using the Bridge method of inductive study (see below for a resource to learn that method). With the help of an image of a bridge, think of the three steps (Observation, Interpretation, and Application) that move you from reading, to understanding, to applying Scripture.

*D*issect the passage by looking up the deeper meaning of words and phrases.

*E*xpress the knowledge gained about the verse, God, and the life application. Choose images, fonts, colors, or materials that convey the message best to your heart first, and then to the hearts of those who might see your art.

Look at our website for my Creative Biblical Expression worksheets, some favorite Bible study tools, and a tutorial with more on the P.R.I.D.E. method and the Bridge tool.

Pam

The Little Details

Allen P. Ross on When David Wrote Psalm 51:

The superscription to the psalm identifies this psalm as David's, written to elaborate on the confession of sin made after Nathan came to him, after he had gone in to Bathsheba...

In [2 Samuel 11–12] David confessed, "I have sinned," and Nathan said immediately that God had put away the sin. God forgave him at the time he acknowledged his sin. So when would this lengthy poem have been written? If we think in terms of the nature of poetic compositions, it would have been composed afterward as a theological reflection on the moment he was made aware of his sin, confessed it, and waited for the prophet to tell him he was forgiven. This lengthy psalm, then, is not a record of what was confessed at the moment of the confrontation; it is a contemplative piece focusing on the penitent's need for forgiveness.[8]

Approach Boldly and Honestly

Only God can cleanse sin and break its power, and to him we must go. David begins his prayer by boldly asking for mercy, and that is what we must do too.

Boldly Ask for Mercy

7. Read the first stanza of Psalm 51 (verses 1-2). What four things does David ask God to do?

David uses three synonyms for sin. Dr. Allen P. Ross explains the differences:

- **Transgressions:** rebellious acts; open and intentional rebellion
- **Iniquity:** going astray; departing from the standard or the way
- **Sin:** missing a goal; missing the standard of God's Law[6]

David no longer sugarcoats his sin. He calls it what it is, and his request for mercy is a request that he not receive what he deserves. The Mosaic Law stipulated adulterers and murderers deserved death. Although Nathan told David God would let him live, still David knew God might take from him the throne, as he had taken it from Saul (1 Samuel 15:26). Like Saul, he had failed to uphold the duties of a king.

8. On what two attributes of God does David base his request (verse 1)?

David can ask this because he knows what God has declared about himself: He is merciful, abounding in steadfast love, and willing to forgive.[7]

For this chapter you'll write a prayer based on Psalm 51. David wrote Psalm 51 to elaborate his thoughts and feelings when confronted, even though Nathan had already told him God forgave David (see sidebar). Likewise, your psalm can reflect a past situation, such as when you first came to Christ, or it can be for a current issue. When finished, it will be your personal prayer psalm.

Now, some wonder why Christians would ask God to forgive a recent sin when he already forgave all their sins at salvation. Billy Graham explains this well:

> When we come to Christ, we have a new relationship with Him: Instead of being His enemies, we're now His sons and daughters! The Bible says, "The

Spirit himself testifies with our spirit that we are God's children" (Romans 8:16).

This is a very precious truth—but it also helps us understand what happens when we sin. Think of your own family for a moment—perhaps the family you grew up in, or your family right now. What happens when someone in your family does something wrong? You know what happens: The closeness of your family is strained, and the fellowship between the wrongdoer and the rest of the family is broken. Only when they ask for forgiveness can the relationship be healed.

But when they do wrong, do they cease to be a member of that family? No, of course not. The fellowship may be broken—but not the relationship. No matter what they've done, they will always be a member of that family.

The same is true for us. If we have truly given our lives to Christ, we are now God's children—and nothing will ever change that fact. But when we sin, our fellowship with God is broken—and that's why we need to confess our sins to Him and seek His forgiveness without delay. The Bible says, "If we confess our sins, he is faithful and just and will forgive our sins and purify us from all unrighteousness" (1 John 1:9). Make this your practice every day.[9]

9. 🎵 (a) Take a moment to ask God to open your eyes to any sin in your life. (b) Reflect on whether you've fully confessed and accepted forgiveness for past sins. (c) If you've previously come to Christ for forgiveness of sins and for salvation, reflect on those moments when you first realized your need and longing for forgiveness. (d) Turn to the My Psalm page at the end of this chapter. Write your name next to "A Psalm of." Then write a short prayer boldly asking for mercy based on God's attributes.

Confess Sin Honestly

After David cries out for mercy, he confesses his transgressions honestly.

10. Read Psalm 51:3-6. (a) In what does God delight (6a)? (b) What does God teach (6b)?

The key to confession is inward truth. When we drop pretenses and excuses, and instead truthfully expose before God what is inside us, then he can teach us wisdom in the secret places of our hearts.

Because we know God is merciful, we can have the courage to honestly confess. The God who searches our hearts knows the truth anyway; we can ask him to show us the truth he knows.

11. What did David know, and what was before him (verse 3)?

Our first impulse with sin is not to see our sin as sin. "It wasn't a lie; just a tiny misdirection." "I was only asking for prayer, not gossiping." "It was his fault for making me mad." "My spouse wasn't meeting my needs, so the affair wasn't my fault." "The sword devours now one and now another."

But David set his sin before him and knew it for what it was. He knew then whom he had sinned against most.

12. (a) Against whom had David sinned (verse 4a)? (b) What had he done in God's sight (4b)?

David had sinned against Uriah and his family, against the soldiers who died with Uriah, and against Bathsheba (at the least, in sending for her—the passage does not tell us how implicated she was in the affair). So why does he say, "Against you, you only, have I sinned"?

Perhaps he refers to the ancient Near East belief that kings had the right to take any woman they desired, even if it meant killing her husband (that's why Abraham told his beautiful wife, Sarah, to claim to be his sister when they traveled). Kings in the neighboring nations wouldn't have thought he'd done anything wrong.

But the God who made him king gave him laws that said, "You shall not commit adultery" and "You shall not murder." The kings in Israel weren't above God's laws. To go against God's laws was to sin against God. All our sins are preeminently against God.

Knowing the greatness of his sin against God brings David to a humble realization.

13. What was God in his words and judgments (Psalm 51:4c-d)?

David says God is justified and blameless in whatever he speaks about him and whatever judgments he passes. David will pray for mercy, but he will accept the upcoming discipline and consequences without faulting God.

Part of the reason he can do this is that he realizes something more about himself.

14. In what was David born (verse 5)?

Our first impulse with sin is not to see our sin as sin.

David doesn't say, "Forgive me because I wasn't myself that day." He acknowledges that he was sinful from birth. He doesn't try to claim his sin was an anomaly and whatever happened wasn't really who he was, and therefore God should excuse him.

> **15.** What confidence does Psalm 51:6 give you in God's ability to teach you his will and how to better follow it?

We need God's help to know the truth about ourselves. "The heart is deceitful above all things, and desperately sick; who can understand it? 'I the LORD search the heart and test the mind'" (Jeremiah 17:9-10). But David is confident God is willing and able to cleanse and grow his people.

> **16.** 🎵 (a) Take a few minutes to pray. Ask the Holy Spirit to reveal any ways you may be excusing sins. (b) Turn to the My Psalm page. Without going into intimate or personal details (save those for your private prayers), skip a line and write a prayer of honest confession and acceptance of God's judgments in your life. Acknowledge truth's importance.

The God of mercy desires to forgive, and so we can boldly ask for mercy and honestly confess our wrongdoings.

The Little Details
Dr. Clay Jones on the Doctrine of Original Sin:

Historically for Protestants original sin has two commonly held components: humankind is guilty for the sin of their first parents and humankind inherited a corrupted nature, since they are sexual reproductions of their first parents.

The doctrine is taught in many passages: "Therefore, just as sin came into the world through one man, and death through sin, and so death spread to all men because all sinned" ([Romans 5:12]); "one trespass led to condemnation for all men" ([Romans 5:18]); and "in Adam all die" ([1 Corinthians 15:22]). So it is no wonder that David wrote in [Psalm 51:5], "Behold, I was brought forth in iniquity, and in sin did my mother *conceive* me" (emphasis added).[10]

David doesn't try to claim his sin was an anomaly and whatever happened wasn't really who he was, and therefore God should excuse him.

Hope Confidently

We've seen two of the six components of David's prayer of repentance: boldly asking for mercy and confessing sin honestly. Today we'll see two more.

When we sin, God wants us to confess our sin to him and repent. *Repent* means to make things as right as possible and to turn from that sin by trying not to repeat it. That may seem hard, but God promises help. Trust him in this: He's good at it. He's been doing it since the beginning of creation.

Today we'll see David put his hope in God's ability to clean and transform him.

Confidently Assert God's Ability

The next stanza mentions *hyssop*, a bush in the marjoram or thyme family. Priests used hyssop branches to sprinkle water and blood on people or objects that needed ritual purifying (see sidebar on the next page).

17. Read the psalm's third stanza (Psalm 51:7-9). (a) If God purges you with hyssop, what will happen? (b) If God washes you, what will happen?

David is confident in God's ability to clean him of iniquity, leaving no spot or stain.

18. (a) In 1 John 1:9 below, underline the two things God will do if we confess our sin. (b) If you haven't memorized this verse yet, make that a priority. Until then, write it on a card and carry it with you so you can review it when you start to doubt God's forgiveness.

    If we confess our sins, he is faithful and just to forgive us our sins and to cleanse us from all unrighteousness.

19. What does David want to hear and feel (verse 8)?

Knowing we've dishonored God and hurt others demolishes joy. "Bones" that "you crushed" is probably figurative for spiritual depression—a crushed spirit dwelling within the skeletal frame.[11] Depression certainly causes physical pain, and many feel it in their bones.

David does not hesitate to ask for God to graciously restore joy, although he knows he does not deserve it. He knows the judgments yet to come will bring pain and sorrow. He also knows if God makes him clean, he'll have great cause to rejoice.

Notice that David does not say, "Cleanse me and I'll grieve and mourn for months to show

Repent means to make things as right as possible and to turn from that sin by trying not to repeat it.

my sorrow." There is a time to grieve and mourn over sin, and even to fast in repentance, especially when we're seeking God's will in righting wrongs (see 2 Corinthians 7:9-10 and Daniel 9:3). But receiving mercy is cause for grateful worship.

> **20.** What does David want God to do in verse 9?

David no longer tries to hide his sin from God—he knows God sees it, and the shame drives him to ask God to avert his face. He wants God to blot out his iniquities from his record book of debts owed.

> **21.** In Isaiah 1:18 below, underline what God can do to our sin.
>
> > Come now, let us reason together, says the LORD: though your sins are like scarlet, they shall be as white as snow; though they are red like crimson, they shall become like wool.

> **22.** ♪ On the My Psalm page, skip a line and write a prayer expressing confidence in God's ability to cleanse you. Ask him for joy.

Ask for Transformation

David doesn't want just forgiveness; he yearns for transformation so he won't sin like that again. In the most passionate of the psalm's stanzas, he cries out to be changed.

> **23.** Read Psalm 51:10-12. In verse 10, what does David want created and what does he want restored?

A *right spirit* is a human spirit that steadfastly seeks to do what's right in God's eyes. David formerly had a right spirit, but he lost it when he willfully sinned. Now he asks God to renew it in him. He never had a clean heart, however, and so he asks God to create one in him.

God wants us to have clean hearts and right spirits, so this prayer is praying according to God's will. That pleases God.

> **24.** What two requests does David make in Psalm 51:11?

David has known God's presence. But in the last nine months, he's avoided God's presence

The Little Details
Hyssop

The word translated *hyssop* probably refers to a plant in the marjoram and thyme family (the plant now called hyssop isn't in Palestine).[12] It's a small bush that bears many fuzzy white flowers.

Hyssop is an apt symbol for cleansing because it was often used for purification acts. For instance, the Israelites used hyssop to paint their lintels and doorposts with the Passover lamb's blood (Exodus 12:22). Moses used hyssop to sprinkle blood and water on the altar and people at the reading of the covenant (Exodus 24:6-8; Hebrews 9:19). Priests used it to sprinkle the water of purification onto people or objects that needed ritual cleansing (Leviticus 14; Numbers 19). At the crucifixion, a hyssop branch was used to lift a sponge full of sour wine to Jesus' lips (John 19:29).

David doesn't want just forgiveness; he yearns for transformation so he won't sin like that again.

----

as he tried to hide his sin. Now he knows God sees his sin, and he asks to not be cast from God's presence. He wants to be back with God.

He desires, too, that God not take his Holy Spirit from him. In Old Testament times, the Holy Spirit was given as an anointing for an office. The Holy Spirit did not dwell inside of believers until after Jesus ascended to heaven.[13] David does not want to lose the Holy Spirit's anointing on him as king and prophet, which was a real threat. That is what happened to King Saul when he disobeyed God (1 Samuel 16:14). Moreover, Nathan told David someone would sleep with his wives in public. That meant someone would claim his throne in Jerusalem, where his wives resided.

> **25.** (a) In verse 12, to what does David want to be restored? (b) With what does he want God to uphold him?

David has known the joy of God's saving hand in many ways in his life. Now he wants the joy of salvation from unjustifiable, intentional sin. He also wants God to uphold him with a spirit willing to obey God. Seeing his own weakness has humbled him.

> **26.** ♩ (a) In Philippians 2:13 below, underline the two things God is working in you. (b) How does it make you feel to know God is doing this?
>
> It is God who works in you, both to will and to work for his good pleasure.

David has passionately prayed for God to make him into the being God wants him to be, one with a clean heart and a willing spirit who can dwell in God's presence and possess God's anointing for service.

> **27.** ♫ (a) In what ways do you most want to be transformed? (b) Turn to the My Psalm page. Skip a line and write a prayer asking to be transformed into the person God wants you to be.

David also wants God to uphold him with a spirit willing to obey God.

Serve Humbly

David has asked for mercy, confessed his sin, asserted God's cleansing ability, and asked for transformation. Today we'll see how he'll move forward and intercede for others.

Humbly Move Forward

Psalms that ask for God's help often contain a vow to do something if God grants the request. This is what David offers next.

> **28.** Read Psalm 51:13-17, the fifth stanza. (a) In verse 13, what is the first thing David says he'll do if God forgives him? (b) What will result from that (verse 13)?

David will use his fall for something good by teaching others the right ways of God and showing them how to return to God as he will have done. He no longer plans to keep his sin secret from as many people as possible. Nor does he plan to hide in his palace so he won't have to face people.

Instead, he will courageously and humbly admit his fall as a means to show others how God can restore them as he restored David.

> **29.** Look at verse 14. (a) From what does David want deliverance? (b) What does he call God? (c) What is the second thing David will do if God forgives him?

"Bloodguiltiness" is the state of being guilty of intentional murder. Under the Mosaic Law, it carried the death penalty. If God will deliver him from that, David will sing publicly of God's righteousness, for in pardoning him God would be giving him God's own righteousness. There is no other means of salvation, for his sin is against God.

> **30.** What does David ask God to do in verse 15, and for what purpose?

When the God of the universe blots out our sins and washes us clean, the proper response is not mourning but praise.[14] When our hearts truly rejoice in the greatness of God's mercy, we will want to let others know that they, too, can receive mercy.

Let's look at what Jesus says about what our response to receiving mercy should bring about.

> **31.** Read Matthew 6:12-15. (a) In verse 12, how does Jesus say to ask for forgiveness for sins (also called "debts" or "trespasses")? (b) Why does he say to pray that way (verses 14-15)?

Pride looks at others as less deserving of mercy than we are, while humility knows we deserve no mercy. Pride refuses to give others mercy, but humility freely gives what is freely received.

> **32.** What would neither delight nor please God (Psalm 51:16)?

The Old Testament Law provided sacrifices for unintentional sins and for intentional sins involving property that could be restored with a penalty. These sacrifices not only revealed that forgiveness came only through bloodshed, but they assured the one sacrificing that forgiveness was granted. But no sacrifices existed for other intentional sins.[15]

More pointedly for David, however, under the Mosaic Law there was no sacrifice for adultery or murder that could restore his relationship to God.

Sometimes we think we should punish ourselves so God will forgive us. But we cannot provide a sufficient payment for our sins, and trying to attempt payment neither delights nor pleases God. Punishing ourselves either treats our sin as minor enough to need only such payment as we can give without the blood of Jesus, or it denigrates Jesus' work on the cross as insufficient payment. David relied on God's word through a prophet to know God accepted him; we rely on God's word through the Scripture.

> **33.** Look at verse 17. (a) What sacrifices will God accept? (b) Sometimes our broken and contrite hearts tell us God must despise us. What assurance does this verse give us?

Pride looks at others as less deserving of mercy than we are, while humility knows we deserve no mercy. Pride refuses to give others mercy, but humility freely gives what is freely received.

Accepting God's forgiveness is essential for spiritual growth. Those who forget God has forgiven them stop bearing fruit (2 Peter 1:5-9). And those who berate themselves with words like "I'm so bad" miss the point of the Holy Spirit's words: "Do not call anything impure that God has made clean" (Acts 10:15 NIV).[16] We should instead give thanks for being made clean.

If we're Christians but have sinned, should we consider ourselves scum until we confess our sins? Not at all. When the Holy Spirit came into us at rebirth, we were made totally clean. But as we walk in this world, our feet get dirty. Jesus said those who have bathed don't need another bath—that is, they don't need to be saved again. But they do need their feet washed (John 13:10).

> 34. ◔ (a) What can you tell others about God's ways and how to return to him? (b) Consider the greatness of God's salvation and how he's forgiven you. How would you praise God to others for these mercies?

> 35. ♫ On the My Psalm page, skip a line. (a) Write a prayer telling God what you want to do because he has cleansed you from sin (for example, tell others about God's grace). (b) Commit to stop punishing yourself in any way. (c) Express confidence in God's acceptance of a broken and contrite heart.

Compassionately Intercede for Others

Our sins affect others.

Imagine being with David as he prays. He's caused those who loved Uriah heartache. His elite soldiers are coming to grips with his disloyalty. He's caused some who looked up to him to stumble in their faith. He's caused unbelievers to despise God as they mocked David's hypocrisy. He likely feels he has lost moral authority with his teenage children.[17]

Moreover, as king he has put the nation of Israel in danger. A king had the ability to lead a nation to God or away from God. If God chose to punish a wayward king, the whole nation would be affected. Since Nathan told David someone would sleep with his wives, in all likelihood that person would take over his Jerusalem palace. Jerusalem was in danger, and so was Zion with it.

David looks past his own needs and desires and compassionately intercedes for others.

> 36. Read Psalm 51:18-19. What does David ask God to do in verse 18?

This is a prayer for God to protect the capital city from which David ruled. God said through Nathan that the sword would not depart from his house, so David asks God to protect the city and its people.

> 37. What good will come if God protects the city (verse 19)?

God said through Nathan that the sword would not depart from his house, so David asks God to protect the city and its people.

The people of God would then be able to offer right sacrifices—sacrifices for the sins for which the Law granted sacrifices, as well as fellowship and peace offerings. All of Israel could bring their sacrifices to the altar and commune with God.

This wasn't his only intercessory prayer. On Day 5 we'll see another of David's prayers as well as God's response to this one.

> **38.** ♪ (a) Prayerfully reflect on those who have been affected by your transgressions. Pause here to pray for them. (b) Turn to the My Psalm page, skip a line, and compose your prayers into a general prayer for those you've hurt, omitting personal names and personal details.

The Worship of the Penitent

For this chapter we've read King David's plea for mercy after he slept with the wife of one of his top soldiers, Uriah, and arranged for the soldier's murder to conceal his own adultery.

In Psalm 51, David boldly asked for mercy and honestly confessed his sin against God. He expressed confidence in God's ability to fully clean him, and he pleaded to be transformed inwardly. He promised to help others return to God, and he prayed for those affected by his sin.

Let's see what happened.

The Results of a Prayer of Contrition

On Day 1, we read that God told David his sin would result in the sword never departing from his house and in someone from his house taking his wives and lying with them publicly. When David confessed he had sinned against the Lord, the prophet Nathan told David God's judgment: "The LORD also has put away your sin; you shall not die. Nevertheless, because by this deed you have utterly scorned the LORD, the child who is born to you shall die" (2 Samuel 12:13-14). Although God forgives our sin, he sometimes requires us to suffer sin's consequences.

The baby sickened, and David immediately interceded for the child. He lay on the ground, fasted, and wept before God, asking him to change his mind. But seven days later the child died.

At that, David arose, washed himself, changed his clothes, and went to the house of the Lord to worship. When he returned, he ate for the first time in a week. His servants were baffled.

> 39. Read 2 Samuel 12:21-23. (a) Why did David fast and weep even though Nathan had prophesied that the child would die (verse 22)? (b) Although the child will not return to David in this life, what would David one day do (verse 23)?

Even though God said the child would die, David knew God was gracious and so he fasted and prayed that God would change his mind. When the child died, he accepted the judgment of the Lord as justified (Psalm 51:4) and worshiped.

> 40. ◗ (a) Has God ever said no to you? (b) If so, do you know why he said no?

As to the sword not departing from his house, David first felt its blade when his son

The Little Details
Paying Fourfold
When Nathan told David about the rich man stealing the poor man's sheep, David said, "He shall pay fourfold," which was the Law's penalty for stealing a sheep (Exodus 22:1).

Some see the deaths of four of David's sons as fulfilling this judgment.[18] Bathsheba's **unnamed child** died. David's third son, Absalom, killed David's oldest son, **Amnon**. David's military commander, Joab, killed the treasonous **Absalom** against David's orders. After David died, Solomon executed David's fourth son, **Adonijah,** for treason.

(David's second son, **Kiliab,** was not in line for the throne. He either died young or David's marriage to his mother, Abigail, was a special type of marriage intended to provide her dead husband an heir.[19])

Although God forgives our sin, he sometimes requires us to suffer sin's consequences.

The Little Details
Old Testament Sacrifices

Here's Dr. Allen P. Ross's summary of the temple sacrifices in the order they were offered.[20]

Purification Offering (also translated *sin offering*): animal sacrifice for purification from defilement and unintentional sin

Reparation Offering (*guilt offering*): money plus animal sacrifice for sins for which restitution could be and had been made (such as fraud)

Burnt Offering: animal sacrifice for atonement after either of the previous offerings

Dedication Offering: grains and crops for showing gratitude

Peace Offering (*fellowship offering*): animal sacrifice and bread for celebrating being at peace with God; a small part burned for the Lord, and the rest offered as a communal meal for the worshipers, priests, and the poor

----

God can bring good out of even our failures when we repent and set our hearts to follow him.

Absalom killed his oldest son. He wept and knew the pain he had caused others (2 Samuel 13:36).

David's betrayal of Bathsheba's husband, Uriah, set in motion the events that brought betrayal back on him. Bathsheba's grandfather, Ahithophel, was David's most trusted counselor, and he avenged his family by conspiring with David's son Absalom to try to murder David. David escaped Jerusalem, and Ahithophel incited Absalom to sleep with David's concubines on the palace rooftop where David had first seen Bathsheba (2 Samuel 16:21-22). It was a blatant claim to the throne, but it was also a grave sin for a man to lie with his father's wives (Leviticus 20:11).

But God protected Jerusalem, just as David requested (Psalm 51:18-19). David got word of the coming forces in time to flee Jerusalem so there would be no fighting there. He left only ten women behind. The ensuing battle was fought in the forest of Ephraim (2 Samuel 18:6), and there Absalom died. Again David bitterly wept (2 Samuel 18:33).

Yet in the midst of judgment came promise.

Bathsheba bore David another son, Solomon.

When Solomon was born, the Lord sent word by Nathan that he loved the child (2 Samuel 12:24), thus confirming his love and forgiveness for David and reminding us all that God can bring good out of even our failures when we repent and set our hearts to follow him.

That was not the only good God worked.

> **41.** Look back at Psalm 51's inscription. To whom did David give the psalm?

He gave it to the choirmaster (we'll meet Asaph later in this discovery book) so the psalm could be sung publicly at the sanctuary. All would hear his confession and hope of mercy. And knowing God forgave King David, they could dare to hope for mercy, too.

Just as my coworker Irene did that day in the photography studio.

Repentance as Worship

Since Adam and Eve's first sin, God has made known to humans how to fellowship with him. He showed that sin separates people from him, that sin has to be atoned for to bring people close to him, and that he desires—yes, desires!—to bring people into fellowship with him.

In Old Testament times, before going to the temple, worshipers were to make right any wrongs for which restitution could be made (such as repaying four sheep for one stolen). Then they journeyed to the temple, where they confessed their sins while making purification and reparation offerings. Afterward they received atonement through burnt offerings (see sidebar). They showed gratitude with food offerings. Finally, they celebrated peace with God in a grand communal meal.

Confessing sins and receiving forgiveness was an important beginning to worship in those days, and continues to be so now. Regularly examining our lives so we can confess sins and turn from them is important. It spurs us to change and to live godly lives that please God and bless others. In fact, Paul rebuked those who celebrated forgiveness in communion without first examining their lives (1 Corinthians 11:27-31).

Jesus told us to incorporate two things in our worship: righting any wrongs we've committed against others (Matthew 5:23-24) and forgiving others as we wish God to forgive us (Matthew 6:12-15; 18:23-35). Jesus introduced our need to give mercy just before he demonstrated how far he was willing to go to give us mercy: giving his own life to pay for our sins. How can we not extend mercy when we grasp the mercy given us?

Worshiping with Penitential Psalms

Find a quiet place to be with God for worship.

Psalm 51

Begin by preparing your heart.

- Ask the Holy Spirit to call to mind any sins you have not confessed. Confess them now and ask for forgiveness as you've forgiven others.
- Ask God to remind you of anyone you need to forgive. Grant forgiveness.
- Ask God to show you any ways you punish yourself for sins. Commit to accepting the complete forgiveness Jesus offers.
- If God has answered no to any of your prayers, follow David's example by responding with worshipful submission.
- Open your Bible to Psalm 51. Pray it aloud to God from your heart.
- *Optional:* Sing a musical version of Psalm 51.

Psalm 130

Psalm 130 is another penitential psalm. Its inscription tells us it is "A Psalm of Ascents." That's a psalm sung when people journeyed from their often distant homes to the temple in Jerusalem.

- Turn in your Bible to Psalm 130. Read or sing aloud the psalm.
- **Praise** God for one of his attributes that you see in this psalm.
- **Confess** anything this psalm convicts your heart about.
- **Ask** for God's help with something this psalm encourages you to do.
- **Thank** God for his steadfast love.

My Psalm

After praying your psalm on the My Psalm page, return here for one more psalm.

- Offer your psalm to God. Read it to him in prayer.

Psalm 103

In Psalm 103, King David shows us that the proper response to receiving mercy is worshipful thanksgiving.

- Turn in your Bible to Psalm 103. Pray it aloud to the Lord.
- Give thanks to God for his mercy.
- Celebrate your fellowship with God.

A Psalm of:

Creative Connection

As I sketch out my coloring page illustrations, I often read the verse repeatedly, each time putting the emphasis on the next word in the sentence, reflecting on its nuances and allowing that word to speak personally to me. Sometimes I stop to look up the biblical meaning of the word for greater depth and understanding. These steps not only help me grow in God's Word, but they enable me, as an artist, to see the words I want to emphasize in my drawing.

For example, as I read Psalm 51:10 for the third time, placing the emphasis on "me," I thought about how many times I've asked God to create a clean heart in someone else instead of in me. In other words, to show them the error of their ways and change them—sometimes, I confess, more for my benefit than for theirs. But the emphasis here was on "me." Create in ME a clean heart, O God, and renew a right spirit within ME. So as I designed this chapter's page I chose to end the word *create* with an arrow pointing to ME to express this truth.

By reading through a verse in this way you will be able to choose which words you want to emphasize in your art. Make them larger, draw them in a special letter style, or enclose them in a banner or border to give them more attention. Notice how I placed the word *renew* in a bunting. To me the bunting represents a party, and just thinking about the Lord renewing my spirit and transforming my life makes me want to celebrate!

So look for the words that jump out at you and speak to you personally. And as you write out the verse, emphasize those words in your own unique way.

⊙ Discover free banner and border downloads.

Karla

create in me a clean Heart O God and renew a right spirit within me

PSaLM 51:10

Chapter 4

Psalm 23:
The Hope of the Lord's Good Care

How does the Lord take good care of us?

Day 1

Introducing Psalm 23

Until my father announced his atheism when I was around seven, we attended a church that met at a drive-in theater. We kids met for Sunday school in trailers.

One day the Sunday school teachers announced we were going to memorize Psalm 23 together, and when we did, we'd get a prize. Every Sunday for a few weeks they said the psalm's words and we repeated them. I caught on that "thou" was a weird way of saying "you," but I didn't understand "shadow of death" at all.

Unfortunately, repeating Psalm 23 only on Sundays wasn't enough for me to memorize it, so when the day came to recite it, my stomach was in knots until they announced we'd recite in groups. I stood with my group and moved my lips, pretending to recite the psalm even though I was actually mumbling only a few words here and there. Thankfully, one girl recited loudly enough for the rest of us to follow.

I was surprised but pleased when I got a prize: a 3x4-inch glossy picture of a smiling Jesus surrounded by laughing children and adoring lambs, all walking among bright green trees.

On a Sunday not long after, my father announced that God didn't exist, so we weren't going to church anymore.

That was pretty much the end of my religious training until in early high school a boy told me Jesus died to bring forgiveness for sins and he was Lord of all. I said, "You've got to be kidding. Jesus? Maybe Moses or David could do something like that because they were great leaders and lots of people liked them and followed them, but Jesus was just a shepherd who liked children and sheep. Grown-ups hated him enough to kill him, so he must not have been very nice."

The message from the glossy picture had stuck with me, even though I remembered little else from Sunday school and nothing of the psalm beyond "The LORD is my shepherd."

Although my first attempt at memorizing a Bible passage failed, the ancient Israelites memorized large portions of Scripture. In fact, some scholars believe quite a few Israelites memorized the entire Psalter.[1]

"Jesus was just a shepherd who liked children and sheep. Grown-ups hated him enough to kill him so he must not have been very nice."

Psalm 23

A Psalm of David

1   The Lord is my shepherd; I shall not want.
2   He makes me lie down in green pastures.
He leads me beside still waters.
3   He restores my soul.
He leads me in paths of righteousness
       for his name's sake.
4   Even though I walk through the valley of the shadow of death,
       I will fear no evil,
          for you are with me;
             your rod and your staff, they comfort me.

5   You prepare a table before me
       in the presence of my enemies;
you anoint my head with oil;
       my cup overflows.
6   Surely goodness and mercy
       shall follow me all the days of my life,
and I shall dwell in the house of the Lord
       forever.

The psalms contain many memory aids, including imagery to develop pictures in our mind's eye, parallelism, and repetition. In Hebrew, the psalms don't rhyme, but they repeat consonants, use wordplays, and have a type of meter. Some psalms are acrostics, with the first line starting with the first letter of the Hebrew alphabet, the second starting with the second letter, and so on.

The ancient Hebrews were onto something important, especially when it comes to what we call **songs of confidence**. These psalms declare confidence in some aspect of the Lord's care. Reciting them builds confidence and instills hope. Memorizing a confidence song such as Psalm 23 means that anytime we need to reflect on how the Lord takes care of us, we can recite it. Consider:

- A teenager deeply convicted over hurtful words he angrily uttered decides to apologize as he remembers, "He leads me in paths of righteousness for his name's sake."

- A man carries the cardboard box of his belongings as he walks for the last time down the gray hall leading from what was his cubicle an hour ago to the exit. Dread grows as each step brings him closer to having to tell his wife he's been laid off. He wonders, *How are we going to make our house payment?* He blinks and forces his mind to repeat, *The Lord is my shepherd; I shall not want*, and *Surely goodness and mercy shall follow me all the days of my life.* His shoulders unknot a little as a sense of God's mercy enfolds him.

- In the shower a woman finds a lump in her breast. A thousand needle pricks rush through her body and out her fingertips and toes. As her heart pounds, she whispers, "Even though I walk through the valley of the shadow of death, I will fear no evil, for you are with me."

When God's Word is in us, we are ready for any situation we encounter.

For this chapter we'll memorize a short song of confidence—six verses that tell us how the Lord takes good care of us. The daily lessons are shorter to accommodate this task. Don't worry if you're not a fast memorizer and you think it'll take more time than you've planned for this chapter. That's fine; take as long as you need. You won't be asked to recite.

Earlier I mentioned that the only part of Psalm 23 I remembered from my childhood was that Jesus was a shepherd. Why did I remember that alone? Partly because the prize was a picture that reinforced that part of the psalm in my mind. The more senses we involve when learning something, the faster we learn it. Reciting after the teacher used the sense of hearing; holding the picture engaged the sense of touch; gazing at the picture added the sense of sight; and catching a whiff of the cardboard when I unwrapped it brought in the sense of smell.

In the Tips for Committing Scripture to Heart at the back of this book, you'll discover how to memorize any psalm or portion of Scripture by involving more of your senses. Use whatever helps.

Begin your study by praying that God will speak to you through his Word. Then read Psalm 23.[3]

The Little Details
Songs of Confidence

All of these psalms can be classified as songs of confidence, even when they overlap with other genres.[2]

16   You Will Not Abandon My Soul

23   The Lord Is My Shepherd

27   The Lord Is My Light and My Salvation

62   My Soul Waits for God Alone

73   God Is My Strength and Portion Forever

91   My Refuge and My Fortress

115   To Your Name Give Glory

121   My Help Comes from the Lord

125   The Lord Surrounds His People

131   I Have Calmed and Quieted My Soul

The Little Details

Metaphors and Similes

A **metaphor** is a comparison in which one thing is said to be another thing ("the LORD *is* my shepherd" here in Psalm 23:1). A **simile** is a comparison that uses the word *like* or the word *as* (the righteous person "is *like* a tree planted by streams of water" in Psalm 1:3). Metaphors and similes paint vivid word pictures that make abstracts such as "the Lord takes care of me" seem concrete.

Metaphors and similes can be stretched to story length. An **allegory** is a long metaphor, and a **parable** is a long simile.

Initial Thoughts

1. 🎵 What stands out to you from your initial reading of this psalm?

2. 🎵 How might memorizing Psalm 23 benefit you?

The Big Picture

Psalm 23's inscription tells us it was written by David. David went from being a shepherd, to a mighty warrior, to an outcast pursued unjustly, to a renowned king. In this psalm, David paints word pictures from his life that describe how the Lord takes good care of us.

We all imagine these pictures differently. Take a moment to focus on the pictures you see when you read the psalm.

Every time I think of Psalm 23 now, the same vivid image comes to my mind: A contented ewe lies in a meadow nibbling grass, her wise black eyes looking at me; the sandaled foot of a shepherd appears to the left; a peaceful stream flows beyond with a path leading from its other side. Seeing this image in my mind immediately fills me with the peace and contentment the psalm as a whole imparts to me when I read it. The ewe's black eyes tell me it's wise to be content with the Lord's good care.

This ability of images to evoke emotion and impart understanding is why poets use imagery so much. If their word pictures paint in our minds images that move our hearts and produce understanding not formerly grasped, they have accomplished their task. If the word pictures are powerful enough, they'll pop into mind whenever we are in need of their messages, and their work will continue.

A picture's power is in its ability to communicate in seconds what would take many minutes in words. When a poet paints an image in our minds, especially an image that stirs our emotions, we remember the message better.

As we study Psalm 23, try to form mental images of what you're reading. When they appear, sketch them in the margin of this discovery book. Rough stick figures that only you can decipher are fine—their only purpose is to remind you of your mental images. These sketches will replace our psalm writing for this chapter since they'll help you memorize the psalm.

The Lord Is My Shepherd

3. How does David describe his relationship with the Lord in Psalm 23:1?

Verses 1 to 4 describe David's relationship with the Lord, using the **metaphor** of a sheep with his shepherd.

4. Turn your Bible to John 10. (a) What did Jesus call himself in John 10:11? (b) What does a good shepherd do for his sheep? (c) By contrast, what does a hired hand do (verses 12-13)? (d) How does Jesus describe his relationship with the sheep (verses 14-15)? (e) Jump back to verse 3. How does Jesus gather his sheep to him? (f) What do the sheep do, and why (verse 4)?

If you know and follow Jesus as Lord, then you relate to him as a sheep with a shepherd. You can confidently claim Psalm 23 as your own, saying, "The Lord is *my* shepherd."

5. 🎵 Read Psalm 23:1-2a. Try to picture its elements in your mind. For this chapter, instead of writing a psalm, we'll draw the elements of Psalm 23 as a memory aid. Turn to the My Psalm page at the end of the chapter and write your name next to "A Psalm in Pictures of." Draw these verses in the box labeled "1-2a." Again, don't be a bit concerned if you're not an artist. Whatever strong image comes to mind first will be the easiest to remember. (See sidebar for ideas.)

   - *Optional*: Add something to this sketch that will remind you of the next picture. By creating links between the pictures, you'll be able to recall them in order. (Or leave a little room to do this on Day 2.)

   - *Optional:* Putting words to music may be the best way to memorize. 👁 Discover music suggestions.

Experiencing Psalm 23 Creatively

Begin thinking of other ways to interact with Psalm 23. For inspiration, review Chapter 1, Day 1. Here are some ideas specific to this chapter's psalm:

- Learn to effectively use color with Scripture in the Creative Connection.
- On Day 5, pick the sketch on the My Psalm page that stands out to you the most and create a visual aid to represent that one scene. Create a more detailed sketch, watercolor, quilt block, needlework pattern, or diorama.
- Carve a miniature shepherd's rod and staff.

6. Spend the rest of your time today memorizing Psalm 23:1-2a. Try some of the ideas from the Tips for Committing Scripture to Heart section at the end of the discovery book.

The Little Details
Picturing Verses 1-2a

Here's how I picture Psalm 23:1-2a.

In the foreground on the left is the shepherd's sandaled foot and the hem of his white garment. His dark wood staff stands just in front of him, as if he's leaning on it.

He is facing a contented ewe lying in a grassy meadow in the center of the picture a little ways back. The meadow is sprinkled with white flowers. In the sheep's mouth is the stalk of one of the white flowers. Her wise, black eyes look at me, inviting me to be as content as she is.

To the right further back is a path leading to a stream of water that flows gently from left to right. (This is the link to the next verse's picture.)

Hope Alive

"Mary Had a Little Lamb" could be my childhood theme song. I grew up on a Suffolk sheep farm in Idaho, and I was a fourth generation shepherd. My first lamb was named Bunny because when she wasn't in my arms, she would delight herself jumping from rock to rock in our pasture. Everywhere Pammy went, "her lamb was sure to go." So when I read Psalm 23 and "the LORD is my shepherd," it is personal, encouraging, and comforting because I know firsthand that the relationship between a shepherd and his sheep is precious.

I will always see my Good Shepherd as my strong, powerful, attentive protector because I have strong memories of my grandfather, father, and brother vigilantly protecting our herds from the ravenous coyotes, wolves, and wild dogs that roamed the high desert near our farm. Wrapped in down sleeping bags with their "rod and staff" within arm's reach, they would post themselves in the pasture with the sheep. It was an uncomfortable, thankless job, but it saved our flocks.

When I read, "He makes me lie down in green pastures. He leads me beside still waters. He restores my soul," that is exactly the experience of my upbringing. I would often walk barefoot through the lush, green grass of the pasture as the sheep serenely grazed. With a Bible in my hand, I would lie down on a blanket or perch on the edge of the creek bank and spend quiet hours communing with God. This was my place of solace and restoration, far away from the chaos my alcoholic, raging, earthly father created in our small farmhouse.

Throughout the years, I have seen how "goodness and mercy" have surely followed me all the days of my life. One could phrase this as "certainly what is good, pleasant, agreeable, beneficial, desirable, and beautiful as well as God's faithful, loyal, loving-kindness will pursue you." Wow! Our Good Shepherd pursues us to give his faithful love and all things beautiful and beneficial. That is why we can walk *through* the darkest valley and not tremble—because the Good Shepherd will console us.

Not long ago, I was exhausted from carrying more of the responsibility of ministry and home as my husband shouldered the burden of caring for his father, who was in a health crisis. As things calmed for a day or two, God created a sweet day off for me in a friend's beautiful garden. I placed my blanket near the lake on the green grass in the cool shade. I opened my Bible to Psalm 55:22: "Cast your burden on the LORD and he will sustain you." I prayed out my weariness, and then looked up what it meant to "cast" my burden. I was to hurl my net out like a fisherman. God was inviting me to catapult my burdens onto his net.

As I continued to study, what surprised me is that the original-language word used for *burden* can also be translated *assignment* or *gift*. I remember thinking, *A gift? Really?* But I kept digging and read that God would "sustain"—he would nourish, strengthen, and support me—and make me sufficient for this assigned "gift." Peace, relief, and a rejuvenating hope washed over me. I sketched out two hands. In one palm was my "gift" of cares, and I placed myself in the other palm. Both my assignment and me, both your assignment and you, are held up by the Good Shepherd.

Pam

Day 2

The Lord Cares as a Good Shepherd Cares for His Sheep

On Day 1 we saw that the Lord is our Shepherd. Today we'll look at how David describes four ways the Lord takes care of his needs as a good shepherd cares for his sheep.

He Provides Good Food

7. Read Psalm 23:1-3. In verse 1, what results from having the Lord as your Shepherd?

A shepherd's job is to see that his sheep lack nothing they need. "I shall not want" doesn't mean we receive our every desire—as we saw in the last chapter, God sometimes told David no. Rather, it means the Lord takes care of our needs just as a good shepherd takes care of his sheep's needs.

8. What does the shepherd do to meet the sheep's needs (23:2a)?

The word translated *shepherd* can also mean *feeder*.[4] In Israel in the spring, good shepherds led their sheep to grassy pastures to feed.

Sheep eat quickly. Then they lie down to ruminate (see sidebar) until the food is broken down enough to be fully digested and absorbed.

However, sheep won't lie down if they're hungry. Neither will they lie down if they fear nearby predators, if they're not getting along with other sheep, or if pests such as flies and parasites are bothering them.[5]

So the picture David paints here is of a well-fed sheep lying down to ruminate in contentment because the shepherd fully cares for his flock.

How does this apply to our lives? One way is that the Lord feeds us spiritual food in the form of God's words.[6] We eat of God's words when we read the Bible, recite Scripture, or listen to biblical teaching. When we later bring the words back to our minds and *ruminate* (think deeply) on them, we're able to fully digest the meaning, absorb the words, and have them become part of us by doing what they say. Doing what they say is essential: "Jesus said to them, 'My food is to do the will of him who sent me and to accomplish his work'" (John 4:34).

Just as sheep cannot ruminate when disturbed by predators, problematic sheep, or pests, so we can't ruminate on God's words when we're distracted by fears, relationship problems, or annoyances.

The Little Details
Chewing the Cud

Sheep are *ruminants*, which are mammals with four-chambered stomachs. They swallow food quickly, filling the first chamber of their stomach. Then they need rest to *ruminate*, or *chew the cud*. They return the swallowed grass (now called *cud*) to their mouths so they can chew it enough that when they swallow it again, it'll pass to the other stomach chambers for digestion. Sheep ruminate for hours daily, and they prefer to do so lying down.

9. 🕐 Think over the past month. (a) What, if anything, keeps you from eating of God's words? (b) When you've taken in God's words, what is most likely to preoccupy your attention and keep you from ruminating on them: fear, relationships, or annoyances? (c) What steps can you take to make sure taking in Scripture and ruminating on it are a daily practice?

He Restores Our Souls

Besides food, sheep need clean water.

10. In Psalm 23:2b–3a, how does David say the Lord takes care of us like a shepherd cares for his sheep?

"Still waters" literally means *waters of rest*. They are peaceful waters, as opposed to a rushing river or a crashing waterfall. Here the sheep can drink and be refreshed, and the shepherd can wash the sheep and cleanse any wounds.

David says, "He restores my soul." At times, our souls need restoration. We want our sin washed away. We crave restoration after straying. We long for refreshment from weariness.[7] We yearn for relief from difficult and confusing times.

"He leads me" means we need to follow him to find refreshing water. Occasionally while a shepherd is leading his flock to clean water, some sheep turn aside to polluted pools.[8] Likewise, some people turn aside to unsatisfying pools to quench their soul's thirst. When we chase the pools the world values—people, possessions, positions, and pleasures—we become ensnared by the "do this, do that" of this world: capturing the attention of the right people; buying the right fashions, cars, and homes; climbing to top positions; and indulging in only the best cuisines, perfumes, and locales. These worldly rules and expectations promise rest when you reach the top, but they don't deliver. They ensnare and injure.

11. 🕐 When the Lord is leading you to his still waters, what pools are you most tempted to turn aside to: people, possessions, positions, or pleasures?

Occasionally while a shepherd is leading his flock to clean water, some sheep turn aside to polluted pools. Likewise, some people turn aside to unsatisfying pools to quench their soul's thirst.

He Leads Us in Right Directions

12. (a) In Psalm 23:3b, how does the Lord take care of us like a shepherd cares for his sheep? (b) Why (3c)?

"Paths of righteousness" could also be translated *right paths*. When the Lord leads, the paths are always the right ones to take us where we should be going, and they're also righteous paths.

Sheep don't choose the right paths naturally. According to sheepherder Phillip Keller, they'll take the same paths repeatedly until their hooves create gullies and their overgrazing leaves their fields barren and infested.[9] A good shepherd regularly leads his flock to fresh pastures so the meadows grow back and parasites die.

We don't choose right paths naturally either: "We all, like sheep, have gone astray, each of us has turned to his own way" (Isaiah 53:6 NIV).

How well a shepherd cared for his sheep would make or break his reputation. The Lord leads us "for his name's sake." All creation watches.

13. 🎵 Read Psalm 23:2b-3 while trying to picture all its elements in your mind. Turn to the My Psalm page and draw these verses in the box labeled "2b-3." Try to think of a way to link this image to the next. See the sidebar for ideas.

14. Spend the rest of today's time memorizing Psalm 23:1-3 using some of the ideas from the Tips for Committing Scripture to Heart section at the end of the book or any other methods you have found to be useful.

The Little Details
Picturing Verses 2b-3

A path leads to a gentle stream flowing from left to right. A small wooden bridge passes over the water.

On the other side of the stream, a shepherd walks along a path that leads from the stream leftward. The shepherd has a staff in his right hand, and a wooden club hangs from his belt. The sheep walks with him in perfect trust.

The path leads toward purple mountains in the distant left. Their sharp peaks surround a deep, shadowed fissure. (This is the link to the next verse.)

The Lord Cares as a Close Companion in Dark Valleys

When I was a child, I wanted a dog like Lassie. She could rescue me if a river swept me away, attack bad people if they tried to harm me, and run for help if I were trapped in a collapsed mine, just like I saw Lassie do for Timmy each week on television.

But it wasn't a Lassie I needed, then as a child or later as an adult. I needed, and have, the Good Shepherd. This Shepherd knows my heart and thoughts, as well as the heart and thoughts of all around me who might wish me harm. This Shepherd created me, loves me, and has a plan for me. Although I didn't yet know him as a child, this Shepherd was already laying the groundwork to later reveal himself to me.

He Is with Us

In Psalm 23:4, David switches from meditating about the Lord to talking to the Lord.

> **15.** Read Psalm 23:4. Through what did the psalmist sometimes walk?

The Hebrew term translated "valley" describes a deep ravine or gorge.[10] In them, dark shadows sometimes hid deadly wolves, lions, bears, or robbers. Yet sometimes the way to and from green pastures and peaceful waters was through shadowy canyons. David treaded such dangerous terrain during his youth as a shepherd, in his twenties while fleeing the jealous King Saul, and as king during battles.

Psalm 23 is often quoted at funerals with "walk through the valley of the shadow of death" a symbol of dying. Mourners hear "you are with me" as both Jesus being with the loved one who is passing from this life to the next and Jesus being with those who have lost a loved one to death.

But this passage isn't addressing only the times we face physical death. He is with us, comforting and calling, when we face the death of security after losing a job, the death of abilities as we age, the death of friendships, and the death of dreams. He is with us, guiding and helping, when we "put to death" sexual immorality, impurity, passion, evil desire, and covetousness, as Colossians 3:5 urges us.

> **16.** 🌙 (a) What type of death are you facing right now? (b) Describe any fears that accompany this death.

God is with us, comforting and calling, when we face the death of security after losing a job; the death of abilities as we age; the death of friendships; and the death of dreams. He is with us, guiding and helping, when we "put to death" sexual immorality, impurity, passion, evil desire, and covetousness.

17. (a) In Psalm 23:4, what did David say he would not do when walking through the valley? (b) Why not?

It's not that David was never afraid: He was. But he prayed, "When I am afraid, I put my trust in you" (Psalm 56:3). That trust enabled him to walk through the dark valleys through which the Lord led him.

What is it about this Shepherd that overcomes fear? His presence unfailing, almighty, and all good!

We will encounter dark valleys of evil and difficulties we don't understand. When we do, we needn't fear evil, because the Lord is with us. No being can snatch us out of his hand.

His Rod and Staff Comfort Us

David found comfort in two implements the Shepherd carries.

18. In Psalm 23:4, what comforts David?

Let's look more closely at these shepherd's tools because they tell us much about how the Good Shepherd cares for us.

His Rod Comforts

The shepherd's thick wooden rod had many uses.

- Even today shepherds in some countries use rods to protect their sheep by skillfully hurling them at bears, wolves, and lions, or by clubbing snakes.[11] *We can take comfort in knowing he will protect us from enemies (John 10:11).*
- Shepherds use their rod to discipline sheep that persist in disobeying.[12] *We can take comfort in knowing he will correct us when we persist in disobedience (Proverbs 3:11-12).*
- As sheep go through the gate of the sheepfold, the shepherd counts them as they "pass under the rod," making sure none is missing.[13] *We can take comfort in knowing our Shepherd will bring us back if we stray (Ezekiel 34:16).*
- As the sheep pass under the rod, the shepherd examines them for parasites and injuries.[14] *We can take comfort in knowing he knows and tends to our wounds (Ezekiel 34:16).*

What is it about this Shepherd that overcomes fear? His presence unfailing, almighty, and all good!

The Little Details

Picturing Verse 4

Jesus walks on a mountain path with a lamb close by his side. The mountain's side rises steeply to the right—there is no way up. On the left it drops into a gorge so shadowed that the bottom cannot be seen. The only way to get through the mountains is to stay on the path. The path's sharp turns keep the lamb from seeing what's ahead, but he trusts the Lord to safely lead the way.

From within the gorge, shadowy figures rise to mock and threaten. The lamb looks at them and presses close to Jesus' leg.

The far side of the cleft rises abruptly, blocking light from the valley. Far ahead in the distance, though, light breaks above the peaks, giving hope that the sun will shine there at the end of the path. (This links to the next picture.)

19. ♪ Which of these aspects of the Shepherd's rod comforts you most today? Why?

His Staff Comforts

The shepherd's staff is long and slender with a crook on one end. The shepherd uses it for support and to help manage the sheep.

- A shepherd uses the tip of the staff to guide sheep in the right path, away from poisonous plants, polluted ponds, and perilous precipices.[15] *We can take comfort in knowing he will guide us away from danger (Isaiah 30:21).*
- A shepherd uses the crook of his staff to rescue sheep from brambles and dangerous waters.[16] *We can take comfort in knowing he will rescue us when we fall (Psalm 37:23-24).*
- A shepherd lifts newborn lambs with his staff and places them at the side of their mothers.[17] *We can take comfort in knowing he tenderly cares for the young and weak (Isaiah 40:11).*
- A shepherd uses his staff to draw his sheep close to him.[18] *We can take comfort in knowing that through another wooden beam, he draws us close to him (John 12:32).*

20. ♪ Which of these aspects of the Shepherd's staff comforts you most today? Why?

21. ♫ Read Psalm 23:4 again, picturing it in your mind. Turn to the My Psalm page and sketch the verse in the box labeled "4." See the sidebar for ideas.

22. Spend your remaining time memorizing Psalm 23:1-4.

The Lord Cares as a Lavish Host Cares for an Honored Guest

In Psalm 23:5, David changes to a new metaphor: a lavish host honoring a guest with a banquet.

The Lord Will Honor Us in Our Enemies' Presence

23. Read Psalm 23:5. (a) What does the Lord prepare? (b) Who witnesses this? (c) What does the Lord do to David's head? (d) How does the Lord treat David's cup?

David's enemies see him being honored and know he's under the Host's protection. When David was young, King Saul saw how much God blessed David and how the people revered him. Jealous, he plotted to kill David. But time and again God protected David, and Saul realized God would crown David king (1 Samuel 24:20).

In the ancient Near East, kings were called *shepherds*, so David may picture God as a great Shepherd King celebrating a covenant being made with his subject king. Such covenants entailed the great king (suzerain) promising to protect the lesser king (vassal), and the lesser king promising to submit to the greater king's rule. The subject king's enemies then knew attacking the subject king was tantamount to attacking the great king.

The Lord Lavishes Blessings on Us

David says, "You anoint my head with oil; my cup overflows."

Palestine is dry much of the year and prone to scorching windstorms. In ancient Israel, no one carried tubes of date-scented lip balm or SPF 30 sunscreen. So lavish hosts offered their guests perfumed olive oil[19] to moisturize their parched faces and windblown hair, plenty of water to quench their thirst, and abundant wine at the table. A cup that overflows describes a generous host meeting every desire of the guest he warmly welcomes.

24. 🎵 What blessing did the Lord give you this week?

25. 🎵 Read Psalm 23:5 while trying to picture its elements. Turn to the My Psalm page and sketch the verse in the box labeled "5." See the sidebar for ideas.

The Little Details

Picturing Verse 5

A wooden table is set before a tent made of red leather. A canopy of red silk shades the table.

To the right rises the mountain range through which the path passed as it led from the meadow to the tabernacle. In the rocky shadows at the foot of the mountain lurk the enemies that had taunted David along the path. They cannot go near the tent, but can only watch the proceedings they had wished to prevent.

At the table sits King David. He is the shepherd from the second picture, for he is both shepherd and sheep—a type of the Christ and a type of us.

His garments are richly ornamented and he wears a bronze breastplate. His head shines with a splash of oil and he raises his golden goblet to toast the unseen host outside the picture. He smiles, satisfied.

To the left peeks a path. (This links to the next verse.)

The Little Details
Mesas and Manure

In his book *A Shepherd Looks at Psalm 23*, Phillip Keller continues the shepherd/sheep metaphor into verses 5 and 6 by describing the table as meadows on tablelands (mesas) and the oil as mixtures in cups poured onto the sheep to protect it from nose flies and disease.

He describes goodness and mercy following us as akin to a sheep leaving rich manure wherever it passes. Imagine little flowers popping up from having been fed by natural fertilizer from sheep droppings, thus providing nourishment the following year for other sheep. Likewise, we should leave acts of goodness and mercy behind wherever we go so they will bless others.

Goodness and Mercy Follow Us

After meditating on how God takes care of him as a shepherd tends to his sheep and as a generous host cares for his honored guest, David draws a conclusion.

> **26.** (a) In Psalm 23:6, what does David say will surely follow him? (b) For how long will this last? (c) What will he do?

The word translated "follow" is usually translated *pursue*. So instead of enemies pursuing us, goodness and mercy pursue us. The psalmist uses **personification**, which is representing something abstract in human form.

"Goodness" reminds us of all the good things David has already said the Lord gives him. The word translated "mercy" here can also mean *loyal love* or *loving-kindness*.[20]

Goodness and mercy follow God's people in two ways. First, the Lord pours his goodness and mercy out to us—they pursue us. Second, we pour goodness and mercy out to others—we spread them.

> **27.** ♪ Think of a current hardship. How does remembering that the Lord sends goodness and mercy after you help in this situation?

The House of the Lord

The last line of the psalm says, "I shall dwell in [or return to] the house of the Lord forever."

Where could David go to hear the teaching on which he could meditate, like a sheep ruminating on grass? Where could he go to listen to choirs sing psalms that would restore his spirit? Where did he go to offer sacrifices for forgiveness of sins? Where could he pray for guidance in paths of righteousness? Where could he go to worship the One who was always with him? Where could he go to give thanks for the Lord's protection, discipline, and good care?

The house of the Lord.

And there he expected to dwell forever.

The earthly house of the Lord was a picture of a heavenly house.[21] In that house are many rooms, and Jesus will one day bring us to a room in that house so we may dwell in it forever. Jesus explains in John 14:2-3:

> In my Father's house are many rooms. If it were not so, would I have told you that I go to prepare a place for you? And if I go and prepare a place for you, I will come again and will take you to myself, that where I am you may be also.

All of us will face times when we'll want to have these verses tucked in our heart so we can speak them at any moment. Having Psalm 23 hidden in your heart will prepare you for troubled times today and tomorrow.

28. ♪ Read Psalm 23:6 again while trying to picture its elements. Turn to the My Psalm page and sketch the verses in the box labeled "6." The sidebar shows how I picture them.

29. ♪ We used many tools to help commit Psalm 23 to memory. Which was the most helpful? Why?

30. Use the rest of your time today for memorizing Psalm 23:5-6.

The Little Details
Picturing Verse 6

The path continues behind the tabernacle to the left toward rounded hills and an emerald-green forest. Where the path meets the forest it turns and follows along its edge. This is the path of the work to which God called David (and calls us).

David has already passed down the path. Following after him just out of his sight are two laughing, fairy-like creatures. One wears a white dress and sunny yellow sash and bonnet; the other wears a yellow dress with a white sash and bonnet. Their arms are entwined, for they are inseparable.

One carries a basket of white flowers, the other of yellow flowers. The white flowers are goodness and the yellow are mercy. As they laugh and skip, they toss their flowers on the path as flower girls would at a wedding. The flowers will in time drop their seeds, and the seeds will grow the fruit of goodness and mercy.

Remembering the Lord's Good Care

God wants us to remember how he's cared for his people in the past so we'll trust him to care for us in the future. God's desire that we remember his good care is why he told the Israelites to memorize songs (Deuteronomy 31:19), celebrate holy days with feasts, and set up stones of remembrance (Joshua 4:21-24).

It's why he says to lay up his words in our hearts and souls, to teach them to our children, to talk about them, and to write them on doorposts and gates (Deuteronomy 11:18-20).

It's why I asked you to memorize Psalm 23 to hide it in your heart.

We hide passages in our hearts through memorization so we can meditate on them any time. Biblical meditation isn't silent; it's speaking softly to help us remember and ponder.[22] Meditation is speaking the words, speaking to God about his words, and speaking to ourselves ("O my soul") in exhortation to apply the words. Biblical meditation strengthens our commitment to and hope in God. It flows naturally into worship.

When those who find memorizing difficult nonetheless make the effort, they please God like a wife pleases her husband when she surprises him with a favorite though complicated meal, or like a husband pleases his wife when he carefully plans their anniversary celebration. Their effort is what shows devotion and love. It is a gift.

> **31.** 🎵 (a) What hobbies and skills do you have? (b) How could you use one of them to teach or remind people of the Lord's good care?

Worshiping with Songs of Confidence

Today we'll worship the Lord with Psalm 23 from memory. Don't worry if you haven't got the words perfect yet. It's okay to look at the pictures or text if you forget a part.

Find a quiet place to worship the Lord. Prepare your heart by confessing any sin and asking for forgiveness.

Psalm 23

> • Offer your memorization of Psalm 23 as a gift to God so it may be used to bring you and others to him in worshipful praise for his good care.
>
> • Open your Bible to Psalm 23. Read the psalm to refresh your memory.
>
> • Bow down before the Lord (if you're able) and close your eyes. Picture the first part of Psalm 23 in your mind. Pray the psalm aloud from memory as best you can, stopping frequently to meditate and pray over the words. Continue picturing, reciting, meditating, and praying through the psalm.

Biblical meditation isn't silent; it's speaking softly to help us remember and ponder.

- Give thanks to the Lord for specific ways he has shepherded you in the past and for the ways you trust he'll shepherd you in the future.
- *Optional:* Sing Psalm 23 to the Lord.

Psalm 121

Psalm 121 is a song of confidence whose inscription tells us it's "A Song of Ascents." That's a psalm sung by those journeying to Jerusalem to worship at the temple.

- Turn to Psalm 121 and read it aloud.
- Reflect on its meaning for your own travels.
- Reflect on how reciting it on your way to worship services might prepare your heart for worship.
- Reflect on its meaning for your spiritual journey.
- Pray Psalm 121 aloud to the Lord.
- Pray meditatively over Psalm 121: **Praise** God for what you see of his character, **confess** anything that convicts you, **ask** for help to do what Psalm 121 calls you to do, and **thank** God for keeping you from evil.
- Close by giving thanks for the Lord's good care.

A Psalm in Pictures of:

1-2a	

2b-3	

4

5

6

Creative Connection

This chapter's illustrated verse, Psalm 23:2, is full of imagery that hopefully brings a smile to your face and peace to your heart. As we read through the first few verses of Psalm 23, we immediately find ourselves in a springtime setting. The word pictures are powerful. They invite us to walk as sheep with our Shepherd Jesus through lush green pastures filled with flowers, and they beckon us to lie down and rest along the banks of a gently flowing stream.

Choosing a color palette can oftentimes be challenging, but one approach is to start with what you know and move forward from there. By doing this you can see how one color or color family dances around your illustration and where you might need to add more of this color here and there to give it balance and weight.

In this chapter's illustration we know we have green grass and blue water, so either is a great place to start. But instead of coloring all the grass the same color, consider starting with the grass closest to you, the grass under the sheep, and use the lightest spring green with the lightest touch. Then with each layer, as you move upward, darken it a bit more by adding a little more pressure, and then changing to a grass-green and maybe even a blue-green just beneath the sky. Varying these colors will add interest and depth to your art. As you begin to color the green leaves, try using the lightest greens for the leaves against the darkest grass and the darker green leaves over the lighter grass to make them pop.

You'll want to keep the blues of the water rather light so you don't cover the lettering, but to add interest here you might color the dividing lines in a darker hue and shade a little from the outside edges inward toward the words.

After you lay down these foundational colors, finishing will be fun and easy with your favorite spring colors for the flowers and butterflies!

👁 Discover more color inspiration.

Karla

Chapter 5

Psalm 73:
Hope When Life Seems Unfair

What should we do when life seems unfair?

Day 1

Introducing Psalm 73

The 75 young adults at the Bible study had all heard I'd miscarried again. Some offered compassionate condolences. More fidgeted and avoided eye contact.

One dark-haired young man with a boyish face approached me with a cheery smile. "I'm sorry for your loss," he said, "but look at it this way: God probably knows you'd be a terrible mother and so he won't let you have children."

Stung, I retorted that plenty of drug-addicted, abusive women have babies, and many women who can't have children adopt and make wonderful mothers. He furrowed his eyebrows as he considered this, but smiled knowingly. I thought, *He thinks I don't want to face the truth.* I insisted, "The ability to have children is *not* based on how good a mother someone might be!"

Suddenly his eyes widened and his mouth silently opened. Then he stammered, "I might be wrong. No, I *am* wrong! I'm sorry. I'm definitely wrong."

His obvious mortification made it easier to overlook the offense.

Pairing condolences with speculations about why tragedies happen is a bad idea. Yet most of us have done so, including me. But such speculations comfort only the speaker who wants to believe life is fair so he can be secure in knowing that if he plays by the right rules, tragedy won't strike him. That's why Job said to friends who claimed his calamities had to be caused by secret sin, "Those who are at ease have contempt for misfortune as the fate of those whose feet are slipping."[1]

We want life to be fair. We want misfortune to befall only on those who've slipped into sin so badly that their feet are mired in muddy malevolence.

But for all of us, sooner or later, life isn't fair.

A single gal remains pure and watches her friend who hasn't receive an engagement ring. A teenage soccer player misses a coveted scholarship when his team loses against a team that intentionally fouls and injures two of his team's key players. An honest businessman watches the promotion he wanted go to a man who tells lies to get ahead.

GOD is the STRENGTH of my heart AND MY portion FOREVER

Psalm 73:26

Speculations about why tragedies happen comfort only the speaker who wants to believe life is fair so he can be secure in knowing that if he plays by the right rules, tragedy won't strike him.

Psalm 73

A Psalm of Asaph

Stanza I

1   Truly God is good to Israel,
         to those who are pure in heart.

Stanza II

2   But as for me, my feet had almost stumbled,
         my steps had nearly slipped.
3   For I was envious of the arrogant
         when I saw the prosperity of the wicked.

Stanza III

4   For they have no pangs until death;
         their bodies are fat and sleek.
5   They are not in trouble as others are;
         they are not stricken like the rest of mankind.
6   Therefore pride is their necklace;
         violence covers them as a garment.
7   Their eyes swell out through fatness;
         their hearts overflow with follies.
8   They scoff and speak with malice;
         loftily they threaten oppression.
9   They set their mouths against the heavens,
         and their tongue struts through the earth.
10   Therefore his people turn back to them,
         and find no fault in them.
11   And they say, "How can God know?
         Is there knowledge in the Most High?"

Stanza IV

12   Behold, these are the wicked;
         always at ease, they increase in riches.

Stanza V

13   All in vain have I kept my heart clean
         and washed my hands in innocence.
14   For all the day long I have been stricken
         and rebuked every morning.

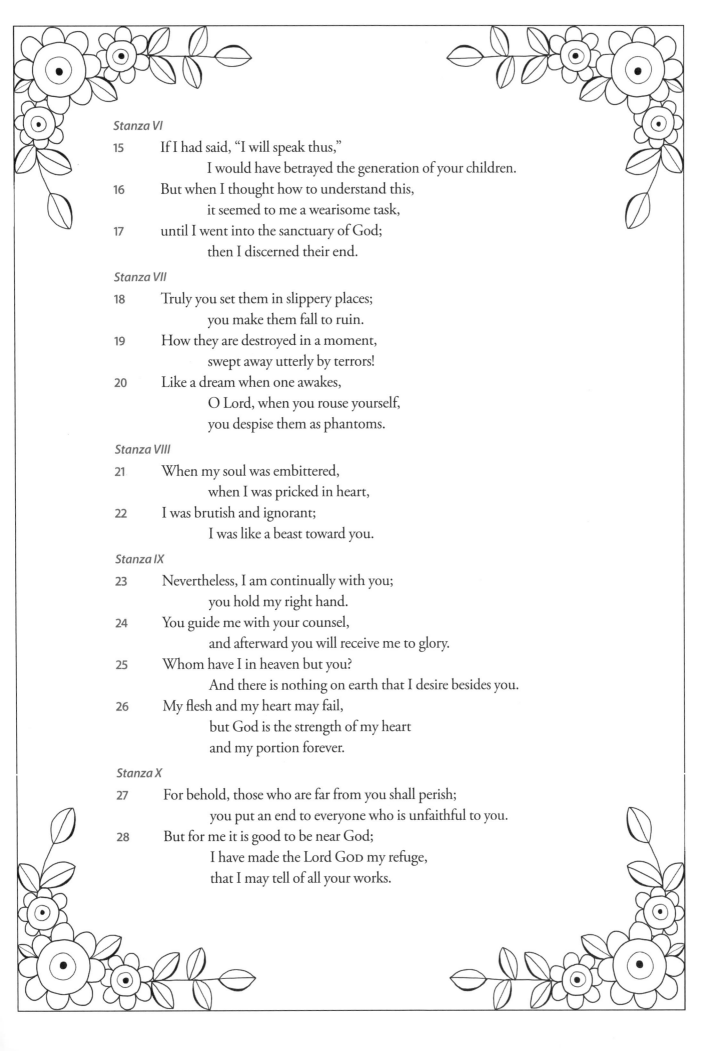

Stanza VI

15   If I had said, "I will speak thus,"
            I would have betrayed the generation of your children.

16   But when I thought how to understand this,
            it seemed to me a wearisome task,

17   until I went into the sanctuary of God;
            then I discerned their end.

Stanza VII

18   Truly you set them in slippery places;
            you make them fall to ruin.

19   How they are destroyed in a moment,
            swept away utterly by terrors!

20   Like a dream when one awakes,
            O Lord, when you rouse yourself,
            you despise them as phantoms.

Stanza VIII

21   When my soul was embittered,
            when I was pricked in heart,

22   I was brutish and ignorant;
            I was like a beast toward you.

Stanza IX

23   Nevertheless, I am continually with you;
            you hold my right hand.

24   You guide me with your counsel,
            and afterward you will receive me to glory.

25   Whom have I in heaven but you?
            And there is nothing on earth that I desire besides you.

26   My flesh and my heart may fail,
            but God is the strength of my heart
            and my portion forever.

Stanza X

27   For behold, those who are far from you shall perish;
            you put an end to everyone who is unfaithful to you.

28   But for me it is good to be near God;
            I have made the Lord God my refuge,
            that I may tell of all your works.

Is there a way to reconcile injustices with God's goodness?

---

1. ♩ (a) Describe a current or past circumstance when life seemed unfair to you, or when your circumstances seemed contrary to what your understanding of God's goodness called you to expect. (b) What kinds of questions did you ask God (or want to ask him)?

What should we do when life seems unfair? Should we conclude God isn't good after all? Or is there a way to reconcile injustices with God's goodness? Those are the questions this chapter's **wisdom psalm** addresses.

Above the psalm sits an inscription: "A Psalm of Asaph." Who was Asaph?

King David appointed Asaph to head one of his three large worship choirs.[2] He was the choirmaster during David's reign, so the psalms by David that say "To the choirmaster" (such as Psalm 51) went to him to be made part of sanctuary worship.[3] Asaph was a skilled musician, songwriter, singer, and prophet. He was also a Levite, the tribe that served at the tabernacle and temple. David gave Asaph psalms he wrote so Asaph could put them to music.

After his death, Asaph's descendants served as the temple's worship leaders. The 12 psalms ascribed to Asaph were written by either David's appointee or one of Asaph's descendants.

In this psalm, Asaph describes how life's injustices tested his faith and the steps he took to regain hope. Begin your study by reading Psalm 73 and by praying that God will speak to you through his Word.[4]

Initial Thoughts

2. ♩ What stands out to you from your initial reading of this psalm?

The Big Picture

By openly sharing his struggle and the help he found, Asaph helped others not only with the answers he discovered, but with the assurance that they aren't alone in their struggles. He also left us a guide to follow whenever we have unanswered questions.

3. Read 2 Corinthians 1:4 below. (a) Underline the reason this verse gives for why a godly worship leader might record a past weakness in a song for others to hear. (b) Why does such openness take courage?

   [God] comforts us in all our affliction, so that we may be able to comfort those who are in any affliction, with the comfort with which we ourselves are comforted by God.

Let's dive into Psalm 73.

Faith Proclaimed

Asaph begins his psalm with what he learned from his struggle.

> 4. (a) In Psalm 73:1, to whom is God good? (b) How confident is Asaph of this?

Asaph says "truly" because his trials at first caused him to doubt that truth. But in the end they gave him a deeper confidence in that truth than he previously had.

In those days, "Israel" described the people belonging to God. Today we can apply this verse to Christians since we're all "a chosen race, a royal priesthood…a people for his own possession" (1 Peter 2:9).

The "pure in heart" are those who try to walk according to God's ways with undivided devotion to him, including in thoughts and attitudes.

> 5. In Romans 8:28 below, underline those for whom God works all things together for good.
>
> We know that for those who love God all things work together for good, for those who are called according to his purpose.

Confusion Shakes Hope

Asaph next describes how his hope in God's goodness wavered.

> 6. What almost happened to Asaph (Psalm 73:2)?

> 7. (a) What caused Asaph to nearly fall (verse 3)? (b) How does he describe those he envied? (c) What do they have that Asaph lacked?

We'll see what he means by "prosperity" on Day 2. And we'll dive into the question, *Why do good things happen to bad people?*

> 8. 🎵 (a) On the My Psalm page at the end of this chapter, write your name next to "A Psalm of." (b) Using Psalm 73:1 as a guide, write a one-line prayer expressing your confidence that God works all things together for good for you (as we saw

The Little Details
Book III

Psalm 73 introduces Book III, a collection that grapples with tough questions. Several of its psalms (74, 79, 89) mourn the burning of the temple, the exile of the people, and the demise of the monarchy, all of which happened in 586 BC. Thus Book III may have been assembled during the difficult, 70-year exile during which Jews wrestled with great loss and unmet expectations.

in Romans 8:28 above). (c) Skip a line. Using Psalm 73:2-3 as a guide, briefly describe a time you didn't know this truth, either a time before you came to know Christ as Savior or a time you were confused about whether God's actions seemed good.

Experiencing Psalm 73 Creatively

Begin thinking of other ways to interact with Psalm 73. For inspiration, review Chapter 1, Day 1. Here are some ideas specific to this chapter's psalm:

- Fast from media for one day to avoid anything that stirs envy.
- Create something that reminds you of heaven and heavenly rewards. For example, write a verse over a photograph of clouds or of a jeweled crown.
- Serve the poor and needy in some way: Volunteer in a soup kitchen, deliver meals to the elderly and infirm, or help the homeless with a building project.
- Rework your finished psalm into a poem using parallelism like you see in Psalm 73.
- 👁 If you're going through loss or disappointment, read Jean E.'s "The Journey of Childlessness" online.

Hope Alive

Sometimes life feels unfair! Like the psalmist in Psalm 73, we are tempted to complain when life is difficult. During a recent Christmas season, I found myself complaining because our rigorous ministry schedule coupled with caregiving for aging parents had left us depleted.

My discouragement deepened when we were headed for a significant downsize (getting rid of 90 percent of our belongings) to move nearer to Bill's parents. Bill said to me, "Pam, I know this journey ahead will be costly, so instead of getting a condo (at a ridiculously expensive price near his folks), what if we lived *on* a boat?" (Feeling for Noah's wife here.)

The Enemy fueled my hopelessness with lies: "God doesn't care about you." "God isn't fair." However, my inner grumbling did not improve my situation, so I made a decision to follow the example of Psalm 73 (emphasis added):

Verses 16-17—"But when I thought how to understand this, it seemed to me a wearisome task, until *I went into the sanctuary of God.*"

Verses 23 and 24—"Nevertheless, *I am continually with you;* you hold my right hand. You guide me with your counsel."

So, like the psalmist, I got myself to God's sanctuary: I piped in praise music nearly 24/7, I used my gratitude journal, and I immersed myself in Scripture and was reminded that *no one* in the Christmas story was comfortable. Mary rode a donkey while pregnant. The shepherds left familiar fields. Jesus was born and laid in a manger of hay! How could I feel sorry for myself when the Lord set aside the luxuries of heaven to occupy a cowshed on my behalf? In Romans 15:13 God met me with a powerful revelation: "May the God of hope fill you with all joy and peace in believing, so that by the power of the Holy Spirit you may abound in hope."

When I dissected the sentence, I discovered "God of hope" is one title. Hope cannot be experienced apart from the Creator. Elohim creates everything. And God was longing to give me joy (a delight and happiness grounded in God, not circumstance) and peace (freedom from anxiety, worry, and turmoil). God would give me this in abundance (abounding, overflowing, and in excess!).

This was what I needed to move forward. This awesome outcome was possible only through the power (able, capable force) of the Spirit (*pneuma* or breath of God). My word study on the Spirit's "filling" found a description of a wind that would fill a sail tight so a boat would move forward. God would do the filling and all I needed to do was "raise my sail of trust" to catch his life-giving wind and be filled with the power of his hope, joy, and peace! It's the same life-giving hope the psalmist discovered in Psalm 73:26: "My flesh and my heart may fail, but God is the strength of my life and my portion forever."

If you look up the definitions of key words, one could read this as: "My body and inner person may perish, but Elohim (the God above all gods) will be my sure stone mountain, my solid rock of my inner person (my mind, will, and conscience) and my territory (my reward and my bounty) through all eternity." God's being your solid, stone-mountain refuge is possible when you act on Psalm 73:28: "For me it is good (beautiful and best) to be near God."

⬤ See my Creative Biblical Expression drawings of these verses.

Pam

Feet That Almost Slip

When God doesn't act the way we expect him to, we wonder why. That's what happened to Asaph.

> **9.** Read Psalm 73:1-14. What emotion stands out to you most?

Asaph had expected God to bless those faithfully serving him with more prosperity than the wicked had. He expected good things to happen to "good" people, and bad things to happen to "bad" people. When life didn't turn out that way and others who seemed less deserving had what he wanted, he envied them.

When confusion shakes our hope in God, there's a good chance we believe falsehoods. Asaph's words show four false beliefs.

Falsehoods About Desires

Love doesn't envy (1 Corinthians 13:4). Envy is a sign that we value something so highly that we think our peace, happiness, or value depends on it. We may even think that receiving the object of our desire is a measure of God's favor.

> **10.** ◑ Think about a time when life seemed unfair to you. (a) What was it you desired that others had? (b) List all the reasons you can think of for why you valued this object of desire. (c) What were some of the issues that didn't make sense when it seemed God easily could have given you what you wanted?

Thinking God was wrongly denying him something valuable while giving it to others less deserving wasn't the only falsehood Asaph embraced.

Falsehoods About Others

Asaph earlier told us those he envied were arrogant, wicked, and prosperous. Let's look at how else he describes them.

11. Briefly summarize how Asaph describes those he envied in Psalm 73:4-11. Or complete the optional question below. (See sidebar for help with unfamiliar phrases.)

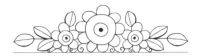

The Little Details
Unfamiliar Phrases

Verse 4: *Pangs* is another word for *pains*. *Fat and sleek* could also be translated *healthy and strong*. (Fat was enviable in ancient days because its presence meant you were neither malnourished nor sickly.)

Verse 7: The first segment can be interpreted several ways: eyes bulging out from fat folds (they eat more rich food than they need); eyes glistening or sparkling from fat (their eyes sparkle over their great prosperity); or callous hearts (fat) bring forth guilt or iniquity (*iniquity* replacing *eyes*).[5] The common idea is that they partake of more than they need.

Verse 10: *His people* may mean *God's people*. Asaph as a spiritual leader would be particularly troubled by Israelites turning to the rich and powerful—but ungodly—for guidance.

- *Optional:* For extra insights into Asaph, summarize his descriptions by subject.
  Bodies (4,5b):

  Self-image (6-9):

  Speech (7b-9):

  Power (8):

  Influence (10):

  Fear of God (11):

  Success (12):

Asaph says the prosperity of the wicked led to pride, violence, and ungodly influence (verses 6,10). He doesn't understand why God would let them have prosperity they misuse.

12. Asaph summarizes verses 4-11 in Psalm 73:12. What does he want people to behold?

Notice Asaph's mistake: No one completely lacks pain, struggles, and ills, and no one is always at ease. Envy is spiritual astigmatism: It skews vision.

Remember that Asaph wrote this psalm *after* he discovered the truth about God's dealings with him. I like Asaph. His willingness to honestly describe his mistakes makes him relatable and helpful.

Falsehoods About Ourselves

We're not very good judges of ourselves—especially when envy distorts our view.

13. (a) What kind of heart and hands did Asaph think he had (verse 13)? (b) What did he think they were worth (see the first few words of the verse)? (c) What does this reveal about his motives for keeping God's commands?

Asaph's obedience wasn't purely motivated by love for God. Perhaps without realizing it, he had used obedience as a way to earn blessings. He thought his clean hands gave him a right to prosperity. God does bless obedience. But when Asaph didn't receive the particular blessing he wanted, he felt God hadn't kept his end of the bargain.

And that showed his heart wasn't pure.

There was another problem too. Jesus tells us coveting and envy are "evil things [that] come from within, and they defile a person" (Mark 7:21-23).

Asaph didn't have a pure heart; he had a defiled heart. Until his circumstances tested him, Asaph didn't know he had a weakness regarding money and envy. But God knew. One of the reasons God allows difficulties in our lives is to test our hearts so he can purify them.

Falsehoods About God

Asaph's bitter cry reveals mistaken beliefs about God too.

14. What did Asaph think God was doing to him (Psalm 73:14)?

Asaph's willingness to honestly describe his mistakes makes him relatable and helpful.

15. Asaph claims the wicked have the attributes in the left column in the following table. List the opposites of these in the right column to see what he means by being stricken and rebuked. The first is done for you.

Attributes Asaph claims the wicked have	Attributes of the stricken and rebuked (opposites of left column)
Pain-free, healthy, strong bodies	*Painful, chronically ill, weak bodies*
No troubles	
Others' respect and admiration	
Power	
Endless ease	
Abundant riches	

Asaph thought his difficulties were evidence that God was punishing him for minor infractions, while overlooking the terrible deeds of the wicked. No wonder he was confused!

16. 🎵 (a) On the My Psalm page, skip a line and list some of your questions during the time you're writing about. Describe your mistaken beliefs about your desires, about others, about yourself, and about God. Try to remember your emotions and let them show, as Asaph does. (b) Skip a line and write whether you thought God was punishing, ignoring, or abandoning you.

Hope that's based in something false wavers. Asaph had put his hope in God's goodness, but his expectations of how goodness should manifest were mistaken. When what he expected didn't come to pass, his hope wavered.

But it didn't fail.

On Day 3, we'll see Asaph move from confusion to clarity as he takes steps toward faith.

Asaph thought his difficulties were evidence that God was punishing him for minor infractions, while overlooking the terrible deeds of the wicked.

Steps Toward Faith

After my second miscarriage, I was certain I wasn't angry over the losses. But when I kept losing my temper over minor irritations, I decided to talk honestly to God. When I poured out every reason the losses didn't make sense, I realized that deep down inside I *was* angry.

Praying honestly helped in many ways. For one, it showed me that some of my arguments for why the losses seemed senseless were unreasonable. I told God, "But everyone else can have children—why can't I?" Immediately I realized many women who long for children are infertile or single. I had mistaken views about others, just as Asaph had.

Other reasons were that I couldn't picture a happy future without children, and that the miscarriages made me feel less valuable as a woman. These were mistaken views about children being necessary for happiness and about what gives us value. Discovering my mistake enabled me to trust God for a good future and to place my value in his love rather than in my abilities.

> 17. Read Psalm 73:15-17. What strikes you most about how Asaph's emotions change?

Asaph was a godly man stumbling in dark times. In the midst of his confusion, he took four steps toward faith. He recounts these at the halfway and turning point of the psalm.

Step 1: Refrain from Sin

Asaph could have turned his back on God, unwilling to consider he was anything but unfair. But he didn't. While he confessed his doubts and confusion, he didn't accuse God of wrongdoing. Although he succumbed to envy and couldn't see benefits to righteous living, he nonetheless stayed true to God and refrained from sin.

> 18. (a) What did Asaph refuse to do in Psalm 73:15? (b) Why is expressing doubts and confusion to the spiritually young a betrayal? (c) What does the fact that Asaph cared about others' faith tell us about him?

Discovering my mistake enabled me to trust God for a good future and to place my value in his love rather than in my abilities.

When we're in a dark place, it's good to get counsel from mature spiritual leaders who can guide us. But dumping doubts on the spiritually young bruises them. Asaph remembered his duty to those God had placed under his care and did not betray that duty.

Step 2: Seek Understanding

Asaph didn't hide his confusion from God. Neither did he insist his instincts must be correct.

> **19.** (a) What did Asaph try to do (verse 16)? (b) How did that initially feel?

He sought answers even though thinking things through was hard.

Step 3: Draw Near to God

Instead of turning from God, Asaph turned toward him.

> **20.** Where did Asaph go next (verse 17)?

This was a place of teaching and worship—a place to draw near to God. He knew a truth the apostle James would one day declare: "Draw near to God, and he will draw near to you" (James 4:8).

Step 4: Consider Eternity

Near God, Asaph considered something he had overlooked.

> **21.** (a) What did Asaph discern about the wicked (verse 17)? (b) Jump ahead to verse 24b. What did Asaph realize about himself?

Until then, he had looked at the wicked only "until death" (verse 4). He saw his problems as "all the day long" and "every morning" (verse 14). He'd forgotten eternity's place in God's scheme.

The view from eternity taught him important truths we'll see in the lesson for Day 4.

> **22.** 🎵 (a) On the My Psalm page, skip a space and write a one-line prayer about what might have happened if you hadn't drawn near to God in the situation you're writing about. (b) Write a line expressing your emotions at the time. (c) Finish with a line explaining how you drew near to God.

Dumping doubts on the spiritually young bruises them.

23. 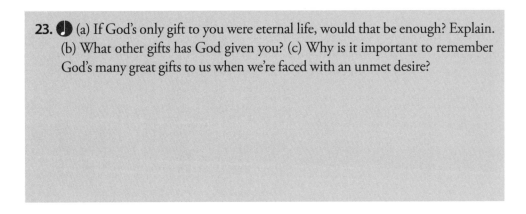 (a) If God's only gift to you were eternal life, would that be enough? Explain. (b) What other gifts has God given you? (c) Why is it important to remember God's many great gifts to us when we're faced with an unmet desire?

Truths Seen

There in the sanctuary, light shone in the darkness and Asaph saw answers. The problem wasn't that God lacked goodness and fairness, but that Asaph mistook how they should manifest.

> **24.** Read Psalm 73:18-26. How do Asaph's emotions shift?

Drawing near to God brings us into his light where we can see truth. Asaph saw four truths—some perhaps new, others old truths seen in a deeper way.

The Truth About Others

The wicked thought God would not hold them accountable, and Asaph feared they were right since he hadn't to date.

> **25.** In verse 17, Asaph said he discerned the end of the wicked. What was it (verses 73:18-19)?

Sometimes that end comes in this lifetime. Always it comes on judgment day.

> **26.** (a) What did Asaph now realize (verse 20)? (b) When God acted, what would his attitude be toward the wicked?
>
> - *Optional:* If God despises as fantasies the false claims, scoffing, and malicious speech of the wicked, how should we regard such words when they're aimed at us?

The Truth About Ourselves

Asaph learned truths about himself too.

> **27.** What had been the condition of Asaph's soul and heart (verse 73:21)?

The problem wasn't that God lacked goodness and fairness, but that Asaph mistook how they should manifest.

When we think we deserve what others have, we quickly grow bitter.[6]

> **28.** What was Asaph like when bitterness engulfed him (verse 73:22)?

Beasts are irrational animals that act on instinct rather than on reason and revelation. But Asaph sought revelation, even if it revealed unflattering truths.

The Truth About God

Asaph now saw blessings he'd been blind to.

> **29.** ◑ (a) According to Psalm 73:23, did God leave Asaph when he struggled with questions? (b) When Asaph's steps started to slip, what did God do? (c) How does this comfort you?

> **30.** (a) What was God presently doing for Asaph (73:24)? (b) How had this kept Asaph from stumbling? (c) How has Asaph's view changed from verse 14? (d) What will God one day do (verse 24)?

The Truth About What's Valuable

> **31.** (a) According to Psalm 73:25, what does Asaph have in heaven? (b) What does Asaph now desire on earth? (c) How has he changed (compare to verse 3)?

When we think we deserve what others have, we quickly grow bitter.

The earthly riches Asaph had formerly coveted were nothing compared to the riches he had in God. Riches on earth can last at most for a lifetime, but the glorious riches of heaven endure forever.[7]

Asaph's greatest desire was for God. Although for a while he lacked his lesser desires, God gave him his greatest.

> **32.** Look at Psalm 73:26. (a) Why is looking to health to meet our needs unwise? (b) How will God provide for Asaph? (c) For how long will God do this?

"God is...my portion" means *God is the provider for my needs* (see sidebar).

When we stop seeing what we desire as providing for our needs, and instead trust God to be the One who provides all we need, envy thaws.

Asaph trusted in God as his provider. And this is what we must do when life seems unfair.

- The single gal continues to remain pure, draws near to God, remembers God will reward her purity in heaven, and looks to God to provide for the needs in her heart.

- The teenage soccer player refuses to break rules, draws near to God, knows what he'll gain in eternity is greater than any earthly trophy, and trusts that the God who directs his steps has a better plan than the missed scholarship.

- The businessman holds on to his honesty, draws near to God, is assured God will reward his honesty, and rests knowing the God whose plans for him are good did not have that promotion within those good plans.

> **33.** 🌙 (a) What is something you've desired, but God hasn't given you so far? (b) How can the lessons Asaph learned help you address these unmet desires?

> **34.** 🎵 (a) On the My Psalm page, skip a line and write a prayer about the truths that replaced the false beliefs you previously held. (b) End with a prayer about how God provides for you now and in eternity. Use verses 23-26 as a guide, if you like.

Truths have replaced falsehoods, and on Day 5 we'll see Asaph proclaim the faith and hope he's found.

The Little Details
"God Is My Portion"

Verse 26: Asaph was a Levite. God gave all the Israelite tribes except the Levites "portions" of land to provide for their needs. The Levites received no land, for God was their "portion." They lived on the offerings the other tribes gave to the Lord. (See Deuteronomy 18:1-2.)

When we stop seeing what we desire as providing for our needs, and instead trust God to be the One who provides all we need, envy thaws.

The Little Details

Enclosure

Asaph uses **enclosure** by repeating key themes at the beginning and end of the psalm:

A   The goodness of God (verse 1)

B   Asaph nearly slips (verse 2)

C   The prosperity of the wicked (verse 3)

C′   The punishment of the wicked (verse 27)

A′   The goodness of being near God (verse 28a)

B′   Asaph finds refuge (verse 28b)

Day 5

Proclaiming Faith and Hope

Today we'll finish up with the last two verses of Psalm 73, discover how to worship through proclamation, and spend some quiet time worshiping with three wisdom psalms.

Faith and Hope Proclaimed

On Day 4 we saw Asaph replace his mistaken beliefs with truth. The lies now gone, he beholds the answers he sought.

> **35.** Read Psalm 73:27-28. (a) What did Asaph behold in Psalm 73:27? (b) How does that differ from what he beheld in verse 12?

That God has not acted yet does not mean he never will. He will make all things right.

> **36.** (a) In Psalm 73:28, what did Asaph now know is good? (b) Asaph previously sought refuge in prosperity. What was his refuge now? (c) What did Asaph want to proclaim? (d) What did he proclaim in verse 1 by writing this psalm?

When our trial ends and we see clearly again, we can proclaim all that God's done for us.

> **37.** 🎵 (a) On the My Psalm page, skip a line and write a prayer expressing to God how the hope of eternity helps you in hard times. (b) Paraphrase or write out Psalm 73:28.

Tests of faith will come. But even when life seems unfair, we can take steps toward faith.

Proclamation as Worship

How often have you been encouraged by the testimony of people who shared openly about their struggles and how God kept them safe and grew them through their hardships? For me, I can't even count the times because they're so numerous. Such testimonies encourage and inspire. Often they show us just the nugget of wisdom we need for our own difficulty. When we proclaim how God has brought us through dark times into the light of understanding, we are worshiping him through proclamation.

You may have found this chapter's psalm difficult to write since it asked you about a personal struggle. But how God brought you through a difficult time may be just what someone needs to hear. Pray about sharing your story with someone.

Worshiping with Wisdom Psalms

Find a quiet place to be alone with God.

Psalm 73

When we read aloud or sing wisdom psalms, we proclaim that we agree with their message.

- Open your Bible to Psalm 73. Prayerfully read the psalm aloud. Meditate on the words and their truths.
- What does it tell you about God's character? **Praise** God for that.
- Did the Holy Spirit convict you on any line? Do you have any attitudes for which you need to repent, as Asaph did? If so, **confess** those attitudes to God. Ask for his forgiveness and for help to know and understand him better. Accept his forgiveness.
- What does this psalm encourage you to do? **Ask** God for help.
- Ponder the significance of God offering himself as your refuge. Offer **thanks** for how he holds you now and how he will bring you to glory.

Psalm 49

Psalm 49 is a similar wisdom psalm. It's written by the Sons of Korah, another Levitical choir.

- Open your Bible to Psalm 49. Pray it aloud.
- Look for something to **praise** God for, something to **confess**, and something to **ask** for God's help about.
- Close by offering **thanks** for the ways God teaches us wisdom.

My Psalm

For this chapter you wrote a wisdom psalm to proclaim something God has taught you. We'll end by worshiping with this psalm.

- Offer your psalm to God in prayer.
- Read your psalm aloud to God slowly.
- Offer a prayer of thanksgiving for what he has taught you.
- Consider sharing your psalm with your small group or someone you think might be encouraged by it.

My Psalm

A Psalm of:

Creative Connection

This chapter's psalm has so many verses I wanted to illustrate, which made it challenging to choose just one. But Psalm 73:26 has a special place in my heart because I memorized it as a young Christian. God has often brought it to my mind to encourage me and give me hope when my flesh and heart have lured me into places of discouragement and despair. As you spend time coloring this verse, you, too, might want to hide this promise in your heart and give him thanks for being your portion and provider both now and forever.

Just as memorizing a verse takes time and practice, so does drawing and lettering. I can't tell you how many pages I filled with the alphabet over and over as I pursued skill in calligraphy and hand-lettering. One way to develop drawing and lettering skills is to begin with tracing. I designed the bookmarks in this discovery book to be the perfect size to fit in the margins of most journaling Bibles so you can use them as a bookmark or color and glue them in your Bible margin. You can also use them to trace the design directly into your Bible by placing the bookmark under the page. First trace it lightly with a pencil, and then go over your pencil lines with a fine-point marker. Let the ink dry, gently erase your pencil lines, and finish with color.

If you are a "non-artist" or beginner, tracing can give you the confidence you need to begin creating banners and borders on your own, as well as help you develop your personal letter styles. Just remember to keep it simple as you trace and add the details afterward. For the more experienced artist, creating your Bible margin design or bookmark on paper first and then tracing it into your Bible gives you the opportunity to play with layout options before committing it to your Bible page.

Discover more Bible journaling inspiration.

Karla

MY FLESH & MY HEART
may fail
· BUT ·
GOD
is the STRENGTH of my
heart
AND
MY
portion
FOREVER

PSALM 73:26

Chapter 6

Psalms 42–43:
Finding Hope When Downcast

How do we pray when sadness overwhelms
us and God seems distant?

Introducing Psalms 42 and 43

She puts on her best dress, catches her straight, blond hair up in her prettiest barrette, and sits down on the nubby couch fidgeting while she waits to see if her mom will make her weekly appointment. Mom seldom does.

She finally gives up and rises to leave. We—her foster parents—ask if she wants to talk about it. "No! I don't care about it. I'm fine," she insists as she marches off, shutting her bedroom door behind her a little too loudly.

That night she hates something about dinner or a stupid class assignment. The next day something at school makes her mad—really mad. She comes home yelling about the teachers she hates and the school she hates.

We ask gently, "Do you want to talk about your mom not showing up?"

"No! This isn't about my mom. It's everybody else!"

A day or two later something doesn't go her way and she erupts into a screaming fury. Angry tears stream down her hot, flushed face and strands of damp hair cling to her cheeks. Clay gently but firmly guides her to her room, and I follow.

"I *hate* you! I *hate* you! I hate the judge who won't let me live with my mom! I hate all of you!"

Her words spew like lava from a volcano until all the hurt and hate and anger are out. Then her fury yields to wails—heart-wrenching wails. Finally exhausted, she stills, her face lighter pink and barrette askew. In a quiet and weary voice laden with sorrow, she says, "I want to sleep." She crawls beneath the covers fully clothed, and we leave, softly closing the door behind us.

WHY ARE YOU CAST DOWN Oh my soul... hope in God FOR I shall again... praise Him MY SALVATION AND MY GOD

PSALM 42:5-6a

Psalms 42–43

Psalm 42

To the choirmaster. A Maskil of the Sons of Korah.

1 As a deer pants for flowing streams,
   so pants my soul for you, O God.
2 My soul thirsts for God, for the living God.
   When shall I come and appear before God?
3 My tears have been my food day and night,
   while they say to me continually, "Where is your God?"
4 These things I remember, as I pour out my soul:
   how I would go with the throng
and lead them in procession to the house of God
   with glad shouts and songs of praise,
      a multitude keeping festival.

5 *Why are you cast down, O my soul,*
   and why are you in turmoil within me?
Hope in God; for I shall again praise him,
   my salvation
   and my God.

6 My soul is cast down within me;
   therefore I remember you
      from the land of Jordan and of Hermon,
      from Mount Mizar.
7 Deep calls to deep at the roar of your waterfalls;
   all your breakers and your waves have gone over me.

8 By day the LORD commands his steadfast love,
   and at night his song is with me,
   a prayer to the God of my life.

9 I say to God, my rock:
     "Why have you forgotten me?
     Why do I go mourning
          because of the oppression of the enemy?"

10 As with a deadly wound in my bones, my adversaries taunt me,
          while they say to me all the day long, "Where is your God?"

11 *Why are you cast down, O my soul,*
     and why are you in turmoil within me?
     Hope in God; for I shall again praise him,
          my salvation and my God.

Psalm 43

1 Vindicate me, O God, and defend my cause
          against an ungodly people,
from the deceitful and unjust man
          deliver me!

2 For you are the God in whom I take refuge;
          why have you rejected me?
Why do I go about mourning
          because of the oppression of the enemy?

3 Send out your light and your truth;
          let them lead me;
let them bring me to your holy hill
          and to your dwelling!

4 Then I will go to the altar of God,
          to God my exceeding joy,
and I will praise you with the lyre,
          O God, my God.

5 *Why are you cast down, O my soul,*
     and why are you in turmoil within me?
     Hope in God; for I shall again praise him,
          my salvation and my God.

The Little Details

Psalms 42–43 as One Psalm

In some old manuscript editions, Psalms 42 and 43 are undivided. Scholars believe they were originally one psalm because:

- they have the same refrain;
- they both speak of being away from the sanctuary; and
- Psalm 43 has no inscription, which is unusual in Book II.

They may have been divided so people could use the prayer of Psalm 43 even when their situation differed from that in Psalm 42.[1]

She sleeps an hour or two. Then she calls softly from her room, "Dad?"

"Yes?"

"Come hold me?"

Clay rushes to her room and gathers her up, one arm under her knees, the other behind her back, and locks his fingers. She throws her arms around his neck, nestles her face into his shoulder. He rocks her for as long as she wants—until comforted, she smiles up at him and says, "Okay."

Our foster daughter feared being disloyal to the mom she so desperately wanted to want her. She tried not to feel difficult emotions like anger and hurt. She pulled away from us and everyone who might glimpse the pain she couldn't really hide...until it exploded against those with whom it was safer to be angry.

Like her, sometimes we try not to feel difficult emotions. Perhaps we fear God or friends will think we're disloyal to God. We tell God and others—and even ourselves—we're fine. We pull away from God so he won't see what's inside.

The psalms we will read today will show us how to bring difficult emotions to God. They are **laments**—prayers about things gone wrong. The psalmists sang laments when loved ones died, when friends betrayed, when losses staggered, when disease crippled, and when catastrophe engulfed. They're the "prayer request" psalms.

The two psalms we'll read today are for those particularly tough times of deep sorrow and pain when we cannot feel God's presence. Originally composed as one psalm, together they show us how to pray with hope when raw emotions engulf us like ocean waves.

Begin your study by praying that God will speak to you through his Word. Then read Psalms 42–43.[2]

Initial Thoughts

1. ♩ Which of the psalmist's emotions stands out to you from your initial reading of these psalms? Why?

2. ♩ Earlier I told the story of our foster daughter trying to deny her hurt and anger. Which of the following ways of handling difficult emotions have you tried? Consider each, and mark those you'd be comfortable sharing with your small group.

   ☐ Deny you feel them

   ☐ Make them go away

   ☐ Nurse them

   ☐ Numb them with alcohol or drugs

- ☐ Ignore them with entertainment or busyness
- ☐ Fantasize acting on them
- ☐ Explode over unrelated things
- ☐ Become frustrated over them
- ☐ Hide them from other people
- ☐ Fully express them to other people
- ☐ Hide them from God
- ☐ Fully express them to God

The Big Picture

Let's look at who the psalmist is and what is happening to him.

3. (a) To whom did the psalmist give Psalm 42? (b) To be able to give a psalm to a choirmaster means he must have had a respected position. Who else is named in Psalm 42's inscription?

This is the name of one of the three choirs King David set up to serve at the house of the Lord. The inscription can be translated either "*Of* the sons of Korah" or "*For* the sons of Korah," so it was either written by a member of the choir or its author gave it to the choir to sing. (See The Little Details on the next page.)

4. (a) What leadership role did the psalmist previously have (Psalm 42:4)? (b) How do his enemies oppress him (42:10)?

The psalmist used to lead people to the house of the Lord, but enemies now prevent him from going there, so perhaps he lived during one of the times when Israel's enemies captured some of her cities. That would explain why he can't get away from their taunts.

Verse 6 tells us he's writing from the land of Mount Hermon, the tallest mountain in Syria. The Jordan River springs from its base. It was often controlled by Israel's northern enemies. Even when the Israelites controlled the area, the sons of Korah didn't minister that far north, so if one of them wrote the psalm, enemies may have abducted him in a raid, denying him his freedom, profession, and home.

5. 🎵 With what aspects of the psalmist's situation do you most relate? Why?
- ☐ Weeping
- ☐ Not feeling God's presence
- ☐ Writing or singing about troubles
- ☐ Losing a position or profession

The Little Details

The Inscription

Psalm 42's inscription has several parts.

Book II: Psalm 42 is the first psalm of the second book of the Psalter.

To the Choirmaster: The psalmist gave his psalm to the current choirmaster to use in public worship.

Maskil: This is sometimes translated, "A Contemplative Poem," but the precise meaning isn't known.[3] Topping 13 psalms, it might be a musical term.

Of the Sons of Korah: "Sons of Korah" was the name of one of three choirs that served at the house of the Lord. Eleven psalms have this designation.

The Little Details

Sons of Korah

King David formed three choirs to serve in song at the house of the Lord. Each was led by a descendent of one of Levi's three sons: Kohath, Gershon, and Merari (1 Chronicles 6:16-48).

Kohath's grandsons included Moses, Aaron, and Korah. Korah was angry that God limited the priesthood to Aaron's sons, and he led a rebellion against Moses and Aaron (Numbers 16). God's judgment came against Korah and the earth swallowed him, but not his sons (who apparently didn't rebel, Numbers 26:10-11). From these "sons of Korah" came the choir of that name that led Israelites to worship God his way.

Heman led the Kohath choir. Eleven psalms have the heading, "Sons of Korah": 42, 44–49, 84–85, 87–88.

Asaph was over the Gershon choir. Twelve psalms are ascribed to him: 50, 73–83.

Jeduthun (Ethan) oversaw the Merari choir. Juduthun is mentioned in the inscriptions of three of David's psalms: 39, 62, 77.

- - - - - - - - - - - - - - - -

Laments teach us not only how to pray for our own needs, but how to pray for others.

- - - - - - - - - - - - - - - -

☐ Enduring taunts

☐ Being away from friends and family

☐ Being in a hostile environment

☐ Feeling trapped

☐ Other:

Praying Laments

Many people think the book of Psalms is made up mostly of praises. But it contains more laments than any other type of psalm.

Laments teach us how to pray in crises. Laments prayed by individuals typically contain five elements:[5]

Lament Element	Corresponding Verses
1. Address and Introductory Cry	42:1-4
2. Lament	42:6-7,9-10
3. Confession of Trust	42:8
4. Petition	43:1-3
5. Praise or Vow to Praise	43:4

Knowing these five elements can help us pray when our own lives are in turmoil.

6. ♩ Which of the five lament elements show up the least in your prayers when things are going wrong? Why?

This psalm pair has an additional element: a refrain found in 42:5,11; 43:5.

Laments teach us not only how to pray for our own needs, but how to pray for others. The lessons for Days 2 to 4 focus on praying through our own difficulties. Day 5 shows us how to use laments in intercessory prayer.

7. Sometime before you complete Day 5's lesson, identify persecuted Christians for whom you can pray.

👁 Find links to organizations that help persecuted Christians.

Experiencing Psalms 42–43 Creatively

Begin thinking of other ways to interact with Psalms 42–43. For inspiration, review Chapter 1, Day 1. Here are some ideas specific to these psalms:

- Find a photo of a raging waterfall. Write Psalm 42:7 above the photo and Psalm 42:5-6a below it.
- Sketch a deer longing for water in a dry desert. Write Psalm 42:1 on the illustration.
- Donate money to an organization that helps persecuted Christians.
- Provide a meal for someone who is mourning a loss.

The Little Details
Laments

Walter C. Kaiser Jr. (Distinguished Professor of Old Testament and Ethics at Gordon-Conwell Theological Seminary) says there are "some thirty-nine individual lament psalms (reading Psalms 42–43 as one psalm)":

3, 4, 6, 7, 13, 17, 22, 25, 27, 31, 35, 38, 39, 40, 41, 42–43, 51, 54, 55, 56, 57, 59, 61, 64, 69, 70, 71, 77, 86, 88, 102, 109, 120, 130, 139, 140, 141, 142, 143

Corporate (or communal) laments are national prayers regarding catastrophes such as war or drought. Kaiser classifies 23 psalms as corporate laments (reading Psalms 9–10 as one psalm). Individual and corporate laments then total 62.[4]

Hope Alive

Bill and I have been happily married for 37 years, and one of the secrets to our success is that we plant ourselves in a Bible verse or passage, or a psalm. Lingering there takes our roots deeper in understanding and application (and in creative biblical expression).

God, in his love, had us planted in Psalms 42–43 during a particularly stressful year when a difficult situation didn't seem to have a solution or an ending in sight. While we waited, stalled in a circling pattern of the unknown, discouraging thoughts loomed: *Lord, I thought we heard you. Why is the answer taking so long?* While we hung our hearts on the sovereign character of God, we also felt as though we were living Psalms 42 and 43 with their repeating cries of lament: Why are you cast down, O my soul, and why are you in turmoil within me? Hope in God, for I shall again praise him, my salvation and my God (Psalms 42:5-6,11; 43:5).

I had three questions: (1) What did this verse mean (because it repeats three times, it must be vital!)? (2) What happens in Psalms 42 and 43 that turned the psalmist from being downcast to being hopeful? (3) What could I gain from the rest of the verses in Psalms 42–43 to survive and thrive in and beyond this crushing difficulty?

As I plunged into Psalm 42, I discovered some beautiful word pictures (that later became drawings). God was acknowledging both the psalmist's and my pain.

"Downcast" and "turmoil" were the emotions I battled. The Spirit walked me through the list of synonyms my study had unearthed: "Why are you downcast, disheartened, despondent, and despairing (curled up in a ball of depression)? Why are you in turmoil (filled with disquieting thoughts, murmuring with an uproar of negative noise swimming in your mind)?" Yep, God got the emotional wreck the psalmist and I both housed inside our souls.

Then comes the command, "Put your hope in God" (NIV). It was a call to linger in hope by waiting with expectancy. However, the key that unlocked hope for me was "I will yet praise him" (NIV). Praise is an active, ongoing action of tossing up, casting out, voicing, and expressing praise to the Almighty God who has answers! The "yet" told me exactly how long to praise: *again and again, over and over, as long as needed—then repeat!*

The results of all that praise would be a shift of mind-set, from spiraling down to lifted up, and I would then see God as my salvation (deliverer, victory, and prosperity).

Because I live at the beach, Psalm 42:7 was my favorite word picture of hope. "Deep calls to deep at the roar of your waterfalls; all your breakers and your waves have gone over me."

One commentator said if you think waterfalls and crashing breakers and waves are bad, God is holding back all the really powerful depths of waters—in other words, it could be worse! It was the waterfall reference that captivated me. I have been under a waterfall. The forceful, tumbling water can keep you down and drown you. But if you move even slightly away, you can breathe again and the waterfall can become a healing tool, like the Roman spa waterfalls. Then, if you move slightly farther out, you experience only the refreshing mist. What God was calling me (and now you) to do is to keep praising him, to move from the depths of drowning in despair on to a healing place. Then refreshment will come.

Pam

Day 2

Longing for God

The psalmist describes his prayer as pouring out his soul (verse 4). His prayer is honest and comes from the depths of his being. It is no shallow prayer that mouths trite adages and hollow praises. Nor is it a claim to a peace he doesn't possess. It's honest. It's gritty. It's real.

> **8.** Read Psalm 42:1-5. What stands out to you the most? Why?

Laments usually begin with calling out to God in some way. The psalmist in Psalms 42–43 has a problem, though: He can't sense God's presence. And so he begins by addressing that very issue.

The Introductory Cry

Verses 1 to 4 form the introduction—a lament before the main lament.

> **9.** (a) How does the psalmist describe his longing for God (Psalm 42:1-2)? (b) What question does he ask (verse 2)?

The psalmist cries out to the God he neither sees nor feels and tells him how much he longs for him. In so doing, he acts in faith that God hears him.

He uses a simile to paint a picture of his longing: He pants for God as a thirsty deer pants for water streams.

He wants to appear before God in the house of God, the place he has known God's presence before. That he is not there doesn't stop him from praying, though. Neither does the fact that he cannot sense God's presence. He asks when he'll appear before God, showing he trusts that this separation is temporary.

Tests of faith are often accompanied by not being able to sense God's presence. Psalm 42 shows us that when we cannot sense God's presence, we can tell God how we long for him.

> **10.** What is the psalmist's emotional state (verse 3)?

The psalmist is utterly honest about his emotions, not stoic. In fact, he emphasizes their depth through **hyperbole** (poetic overstatement). Grief isn't something to hide from God, but to pour out to him.

Emotions can drive us to or away from God. Our psalmist's sorrows send him straight to the God he trusts.

Indeed, trying to hide our feelings from God or pushing emotions away so we won't feel them can be the reason we can't sense his presence. Coming into God's presence requires coming into his light, and that means allowing all truth to be exposed, including the truth of our emotions.

> **11.** What are the people around the psalmist saying to him (Psalm 42:3)?

Not only can he not sense God's presence, but the people around him tell him God has deserted him. The psalmist's enemies voice a lie he must stand firm against. Our enemy the devil tries to break our resolve in this way, but God uses our recognizing and standing against falsehoods in others' words to help us recognize and stand against falsehoods in our own thoughts.

The psalmist turns his thoughts to past times when he knew God's presence, and he remembers leading a procession to the house of God to celebrate one of the annual festivals.

> **12.** (a) With what did he lead others (verse 4)? (b) What were his emotions at that time?

The festivals celebrated God's provision in granting a harvest. The Israelites needed rain and protection from enemies to have good harvests. So he brings to mind a time of joyfully leading others to celebrate God's gracious and good provision.

Recalling God's prior care gives us hope for his present care. Remembering how we've joyfully known God's presence in the past gives us hope that we'll joyfully experience his presence in the future.

> **13.** ♪ (a) In a word or two, name a current struggle. (b) Describe a time you joyfully told others how God had provided something for you. (c) Describe a time when you felt God's presence. What were your emotions? (d) How does remembering these last two times build hope for today's struggle?

Recalling God's prior care gives us hope for his present care.

The psalmist has now called out to God, honestly told him what's wrong, and remembered sensing God's presence in the past.

14. 🎵 (a) On the My Psalm page at the end of this chapter, write your name next to "A Psalm of." (b) In a corner, jot a word or two describing a current struggle you can write a prayer about. If you're struggle-free today, think of a past struggle you remember well. (c) Write a prayer expressing your longing for God's presence in that struggle. Use a simile or metaphor if you like. (d) Honestly describe your emotional state and how you got there, including any mocking words or troubled thoughts. (e) Describe a time you remember joyfully being in God's presence.

Now we come to the psalm's refrain.

The Refrain

Sometimes when talking to someone, I'll forget what I want to say. I'll tell myself, "Think! What was it?" The psalmist does something similar: In the midst of praying, he talks to himself.

15. What two questions does the psalmist ask himself (verse 5)?

These are important questions. Honest answers tell us how to pray.

- *I miss my husband so much since his death, and I can't imagine being happy without him.*
- *I'm angry that I didn't get the promotion I deserved. My pride is wounded and my ambitions are blocked.*
- *God hasn't answered my prayers and I don't know if he cares about me.*
- *I'm discouraged and wonder what's wrong with me that I can't find a job. I wonder if God is mad at me.*

16. (a) What does the psalmist tell himself to do (verse 5c)? (b) Why should he do this? (c) What is God to him (5d-6a)? (Note: the phrase "my God" at the beginning of verse 6 could either end the previous poetic line or begin the next. Since the other instances of the refrain end with "and my God," we'll address it here as if it ends the poetic line in verse 5.)

The psalmist tells himself to hope in God because he will again praise God: He will get to the other side of this struggle, see God's salvation, and praise him for what he has done. He knows this because God is his salvation—the One who will save him in his difficulty and work it for good—and because God is *his* God—the Ruler whom he serves.

Romans 8:28 tells us, "We know that for those who love God all things work together for good, for those who are called according to his purpose." Based on that promise, we can imagine ourselves being on the other side of our struggle, giving thanks for the good God has worked—even if we think being on the other side might be eons away.

Here are words we might say to encourage ourselves:

- *Hope in God, for I will look back and praise him for how he cared for me and brought me companions, and I will reunite with my husband in heaven.*
- *Hope in God, for I will see that his plans for me are good. He's purging selfish ambitions and will lift me up when I humble myself.*
- *Hope in God, for he cares for me deeply and sorrows over my pain, and I will look back and see his loving hand.*
- *Hope in God, for I will look back and see how he was guiding me to the right job.*

> 17. 🎵 Think of a struggle you may be having today. (a) In one sentence, how would you answer the two questions in Psalm 42:5 regarding your struggle? (b) Picture yourself being on the other side of the trouble, praising God for what he has done through it. With this vision of being on the other side in mind, complete the sentence, "Hope in God; for…" (c) What encouragement do you take in God being your salvation and your God in this situation?

The psalmist doesn't go through this exercise just once. He does it three times in Psalms 42–43, making this verse the psalm's **refrain**.[6] We need to make some actions into habits, and this exercise is one.

Try this: Every time you feel sad or disturbed over the next few days, ask yourself these two questions: "Why are you cast down, O my soul, and why are you in turmoil within me?" As soon as you identify the source of your emotions, picture being on the other side. Then tell yourself, "Hope in God; for I shall again praise him, my salvation and my God."

If you don't think you can remember these words, write them down on a card you can carry with you. Repeat this process every time you feel a difficult emotion. You should find your hope building as you face the real issue and encourage yourself to hope in God. On Day 5 you can describe how this went.

> 18. 🎵 On the My Psalm page, skip a line and write one of the following: (a) your answer to the previous question about how you would complete the sentence, "Hope in God; for…"; (b) the refrain from Psalm 42:11; or (c) Psalm 42:11 in your own words.

Every time you feel sad or disturbed, ask yourself these two questions: "Why are you cast down, O my soul, and why are you in turmoil within me?"

Hope in Sorrow

Laments by definition contain a segment where the psalmist pours out what's wrong—the "lament proper." Laments usually hold a confession of trust as well. The psalm's next stanza has both.

> **19.** Read Psalm 42:6-11. What stands out to you the most? Why?

In Psalm 42, the psalmist laments his troubles around a confession of trust. He arranges them in a chiasm, with the confession of trust in the central place of importance:

A   Lament

   B   Confession of trust

A'   Lament

The Lament

The lament begins with the psalmist describing his emotions in another way.

> **20.** (a) According to Psalm 42:6, what is the psalmist's emotional state? (b) What does he therefore do?

When our soul is downcast, when we despair or are depressed, what we must do is remember God. The word translated *remember* here means more than just to call something to mind; it means *to act on that memory*. The psalmist acts by praying to God.[7]

The psalmist writes from the land containing the great Mount Hermon and the mouth of the Jordan River. He is on Mount Mizar ("little mountain"), which is probably one of the smaller peaks in the mountain range.

> **21.** (a) The psalmist wants to hear the praise songs accompanying a journey to the temple. What does he hear instead (verse 7)? (b) What do his circumstances feel like to him? (c) To whom do the waterfalls, breakers, and waves of his tumultuous circumstances belong?

The deer panted for streams of water, but here at the Jordan's mouth are dangerous whirlpools and whitewater cascades. The life-giving water is in a life-threatening form. The psalmist remembers the shouts and praises at the temple, but now the roar of the waterfalls drowns out all else. The tears fall from his eyes like water tumbles down the mountains. The water's turbulence reflects his life's turbulence, and it is from God.

And yet the psalmist has hope in the God to whom he pours out his troubles.

The Confession of Trust

> **22.** (a) What is God doing by day (Psalm 42:8)? (b) What is with the psalmist at night? (c) How does this show his trust? (d) How does this relate to what you learned about using the confidence psalms in Chapter 4?

Always, God is with him. By day he knows God commands his steadfast love toward him. At night when dark thoughts threaten most, he sings a prayer song to the God of his life, a song that came from God himself—perhaps part or all of this psalm.

> **23.** 🌓 Have you ever sung songs or prayed psalms to God on a troubled night? If so, how has that helped strengthen your hope in God?

The psalmist asserts his trust in God, reminding himself of God's love and of the prayer song God has given him to sing at night. In doing so he strengthens his hope in God.

The Lament Continued

Buoyed by hope, the psalmist asks God two questions related to why he is downcast.

> **24.** (a) What does the psalmist call God in Psalm 42:9? (b) What is his first question?

The psalmist shows his faith when he addresses God as his rock, his safe refuge from danger.

Then he asks, "Why have you forgotten me?" The psalmist does not doubt God's omniscience—he realizes God possesses all knowledge. In the Old Testament, "remembering" is equivalent to acting and "forgetting" is equivalent to not acting.[8] For example, God "remembers" someone's sins when he punishes those sins, and he "forgets" his or her sins when he stops punishment. But he doesn't give up omniscience so that he has gaps in his knowledge of human history. When you read about David and Bathsheba in Chapter 3, you knew God didn't say, "What? I didn't know David committed adultery!"

The life-giving water is in a life-threatening form.

The psalmist here means, "Why are you not acting on my behalf?" This to him feels like being forgotten, which is one reason he was downcast.

God's apparent inaction leads to his second question: Why is he suffering the results of God's inaction?

> **25.** What's another reason the psalmist mourns (42:9)?

Oppression is more than just taunts and captivity: It's mistreatment.

> **26.** (a) What do his adversaries' taunts feel like physically (verse 10)? (b) How often do they taunt him?

The taunts are continual ("all the day"[9]), and they're affecting his health.

So this, then, is what casts down his soul. His enemies oppress and mock him nonstop, they tell him God has abandoned him, and the mistreatment causes him physical pain. God could stop all this, but he hasn't, so the psalmist feels forgotten. Yet he knows God is his rock and God's love is steadfast in spite of his circumstances.

The Refrain

The psalmist has poured out to God the reasons for his tears. Now he again encourages himself to hope in God.

> **27.** 🎵 Read Psalm 42:11. When our spirits are down, why is it good to keep encouraging ourselves to hope in God?

> **28.** 🎵 (a) Turn to the My Psalm page. Leave a blank space and write a line expressing what emotion causes you to remember God, using Psalm 42:6 as a pattern. (b) If desired, write a line describing your emotions, using verse 7 as an example. (c) Leave a blank space and write a line asserting your confidence in the Lord, using verse 8 as a guide. (d) Leave a blank space and write a prayer that expresses the reason for your struggles in the situation you're describing. Use verses 9-10 for inspiration. (e) Leave a blank space and write out your refrain.

The Little Details
"I," "You," and "They"

Laments usually draw on the triangular relationship among three parties:

- I (the psalmist)
- You (God)
- They (the enemies)

God is the psalmist's rock and refuge. The enemies reject God and oppress the psalmist. The psalmist expects, therefore, that God will intervene.

God could stop all this, but he hasn't, so the psalmist feels forgotten.

Petitioning and Praising

The psalmist has called out to the God whose presence he cannot sense. He's asked himself why his emotions are in turmoil and he's exhorted himself to hope in God. He's told God why he's distraught and he's confessed his confident trust in God. Now the psalmist comes to what he wants God to do.

Most laments contain a petition and a praise. In the psalm pair we're looking at, these are in Psalm 43.

> **29.** Read Psalm 43. What stands out to you the most? Why?

The Petition

Once we've identified the source of our emotions and taken our troubles and sorrows to God, we can pray for deliverance according to what we know is God's will.

> **30.** (a) In what three ways does the psalmist describe his enemies in Psalm 43:1?
> (b) What three actions does the psalmist ask God to take?

A request for vindication is a request for what's wrong to be made right. When God rescues him, then all will know God is with him. When we've done nothing wrong to deserve the attacks we receive, we can pray for vindication. The psalmist does not have the ability to defend or deliver himself from his enemies, so he asks God to defend and deliver him.

> **31.** (a) What reason does the psalmist give for why God should act (Psalm 43:2a)?
> (b) This is an expression of confidence, but what questions does he have that seem confusing given his confidence in God (verse 2b)?

In the psalms, petitions often include reasons God should grant requests, such as his promises, his character, his honor; the greatness of the need; or the petitioner's desire to praise God for the answered prayer.[10] Being able to give such reasons assures us we're praying according to God's will.

Here the psalmist says he's taken refuge in God, so God should act. He is confused that his circumstances are other than what he expected since he took refuge in God. So he expresses his confusion to God, but without wavering from believing God is his refuge.

> **32.** (a) What does the psalmist want God to send (Psalm 43:3)? (b) Where will they bring him?

Light represents many things in Scripture, including clarity for what we don't understand, illumination of the path we should take, joy, God's mercy, and salvation.[11] Truth dispels the lies the deceitful enemies have told as well as their taunts that God has abandoned him. The psalmist asks that light and truth lead him to God's presence.

The Praise

Nearly all the laments either praise God for anticipated deliverance or promise to publicly praise him when the deliverance happens.

> **33.** (a) When God brings the psalmist to the temple, where will he go (verse 4)? (b) What does he call God? (c) How will he praise God?

The psalmist expresses here his confidence that God will deliver him, and he commits to praising him at the altar. He vows to give a public thanksgiving offering (we'll learn about these in our final chapter's study). Such an offering encouraged others' faith and met the needs of the poor.

> **34.** ♩ Write a praise to God for a petition he has granted you. Plan to share this with your small group.

The psalmist says he'll accompany his praise with music. He will once again lead others to praise God exuberantly. He calls God, "God my exceeding joy."

While still in the midst of hardship, the psalmist sets his mind on how he will praise God for his deliverance and looks toward the joy that will fill him.

The Refrain

Once again, the psalmist repeats his refrain. But this time, when he says, "I shall again praise him," he has his praise planned out.

35. Read Psalm 43:5. How might having his plans for praising God laid out affect his hope that he'll have reason to fulfill those plans? Explain.

36. 🎵 (a) Turn to the My Psalm page. Leave a blank space and write out your petition for God to deliver you from difficulty, using Psalm 43:1-3 as a guide. (b) Leave a blank space and write how you will praise God to others when he answers your prayer. (c) Leave a blank space and write out your refrain.

Day 5

Worshiping in Sorrows

Does it surprise you how freely the psalmist expresses his emotions? In the Bible, even grown men weep publicly, wail loudly, smear dust on their heads, and rip their clothes. People sob together.

In the modern-day Western world, many tend to hide difficult emotions. We keep a stiff upper lip, fight back tears, and swallow anger.

Sometimes Christians equate spirituality with never feeling sad or angry. Yet the psalmists expressed a range of difficult emotions to God, including fear, sorrow, anger, grief, and jealousy. When we tell God the truth about what we feel and why, the Holy Spirit can minister to our needs.

We can express our true emotions to God while still maintaining confident trust in him and while rejoicing in his power and love for us. As Paul put it, we can be "sorrowful, yet always rejoicing" (2 Corinthians 6:10). Such prayer is worship.

37. ♪ On Day 2, I encouraged you to try this: Every time you feel sad or disturbed, ask yourself the two questions in the refrain of this psalm, and then tell yourself to hope in God. (a) How did this exercise help build your hope in God? (b) Did it help you rejoice in the midst of sorrow? Explain. (c) Is this exercise a practice you'll continue? Explain.

"Deliver Us from Evil"

Jesus tells us to pray, "Deliver us from evil" (Matthew 6:13). That is what this pair of psalms is about: praying for deliverance from evil. Since we know God wants us to pray for deliverance, we know we're praying according to his will.

We pray to be delivered from the evil in this world and from the schemes of the Evil One, who seeks to destroy us spiritually. God apparently rescued our psalmist since he was able to deposit this psalm with the choirmaster. But his final delivery was not on this earth.

Nor is ours. Our final deliverance from evil awaits the return of the King.

When the psalmist said God was his salvation, the full meaning of this attribute had yet to be revealed. When we say God is our "salvation," we don't mean salvation just from life's difficulties. God has provided salvation from the penalty for our sins that we may live forever in his kingdom that evil will never touch.

The Little Details

Sorrow in the New Testament

"Jesus wept" (John 11:35).

"In the days of his flesh, Jesus offered up prayers and supplications, with loud cries and tears, to him who was able to save him from death, and he was heard because of his reverence" (Hebrews 5:7).

"Rejoice with those who rejoice, weep with those who weep" (Romans 12:15).

"For I wrote to you out of much affliction and anguish of heart and with many tears" (2 Corinthians 2:4).

"I have great sorrow and unceasing anguish in my heart" (Romans 9:2).

"Indeed he was ill, near to death. But God had mercy on him, and not only on him but on me also, lest I should have sorrow upon sorrow" (Philippians 2:27).

"And [Peter] went out and wept bitterly" (Matthew 26:75).

"And there was much weeping on the part of all" (Acts 20:37).

---

38. (a) According to Revelation 21:1, what will God create? (b) What will then be no more (verse 4)? (c) What cannot enter there (verse 27)?

The apostle Paul spoke of the afflictions, beatings, imprisonments, and false accusations he faced as he sought to spread the good news about salvation through Jesus' sacrifice on the cross. Yet, he said, knowing that God, who raised Jesus, would also raise him kept him from losing heart.

39. (a) What are our afflictions like compared to the glory that will come (2 Corinthians 4:17)? (b) What are our afflictions preparing for us? (c) To what should we look: the things of this earth that will pass away or the eternal things to come (verse 18)?

Worshiping Through Intercession

Laments teach us how to pray in troubled times, as we've seen during the first four days in this chapter. But they also teach us how to pray for others. When we read laments while life is pleasant, we can remember and pray for those for whom it is not. Laments remind us of those facing hardship. This is good, for we're commanded, "Remember those who are in prison, as though in prison with them, and those who are mistreated, since you also are in the body" (Hebrews 13:3). "Remember" here means not just to bring to mind, but to act. Our prayers are one way we can act.

Intercessory prayer is an act of worship and faith. God chooses to act through the "fervent prayer of a righteous intercessor."[13] We see this in the lives of the great Old Testament intercessors: Abraham, Moses, and Daniel. We see this in the apostles' repeated admonishments for Christians to pray for each other, and in their examples of daily praying for the church. We see it in Jesus' model of interceding for all those who would follow him throughout the ages. And we see it in the Holy Spirit's constant intercession for us.

Interceding through prayer inspires us to intercede in other ways. We may donate food to a homeless shelter, volunteer to help victims of domestic abuse, offer rides to the elderly, or tutor underprivileged children. We may support organizations that take food, medical care, and Bibles to the persecuted. Jesus said, "For truly, I say to you, whoever gives you a cup of water to drink because you belong to Christ will by no means lose his reward" (Mark 9:41).

Worshiping with Laments

Laments are prayer request psalms. You can often pray them word for word, personalizing your prayer afterward. Today we'll begin worshiping with laments by interceding for others, and we'll finish by presenting our own needs. In the next chapter we'll continue our look at laments.

Many Christians live under persecution in lands hostile to Christianity. On Day 1, we gave you suggestions for identifying persecuted Christians for whom you could pray today. Bring to mind their situation as you prepare to worship.

Psalms 42–43

Find a quiet place and prepare your heart for worship.

- Turn in your Bible to Psalms 42 and 43.

- Pray through Psalms 42 and 43 aloud for persecuted Christians. On the refrain, examine both why the persecution distresses you and why those you're praying for are downcast. Pray word for word, pausing to personalize anywhere you'd like.

- *Optional:* If you know someone going through a time of darkness now, pray Psalms 42 and 43 for them.

- *Optional:* Sing all or portions of Psalms 42 and 43 to the Lord.

Psalm 71

Psalm 71 is an individual lament, as are Psalms 42 and 43. We'll examine it in depth in the next chapter. For now, notice the five lament elements:

Lament Element	Corresponding Verses
1. Address and Introductory Cry	71:1-4
2. Confession of Trust	71:5-8,14
3. Lament	71:9-11
4. Petition	71:12-13
5. Praise	71:15-24

- Intercede for the persecuted church using Psalm 71 as your guide.

My Psalm

Finish by worshiping the Lord your God with the psalm you wrote on the next page.

- Offer the psalm you've written on the My Psalm page to God. Read it to him in prayer.

- Close by giving thanks for the final deliverance to come.

When we read laments while life is pleasant, we can remember and pray for those for whom it is not.

My Psalm

A Psalm of:

Creative Connection

This chapter's psalms are all about the Word and the words! I designed Psalm 42:11, which is repeated in Psalm 42:5-6 and Psalm 43:5, in such a way as to lead you through the verse, visually highlighting key words and phrases through a variety of letter styles and visual elements. Graphic design has rules about how many fonts or letter styles should be used in any given design, but one of the fun things about this style is that it has no rules! You can combine several creative letter styles the same way you would bring a variety of flowers together in one vase to create a stunning bouquet.

In this verse the big questions begin with "Why?" "Why are you cast down, O my soul, and why are you in turmoil within me?" Instead of repeating the "why" twice, I chose to set it apart by itself and have it point to both questions almost as if they were one, because in essence they are. Both represent a state of being we find ourselves in when we are not putting our hope in God.

We all talk to ourselves, don't we? Notice the arrow from the question to the one being questioned. Yes, the psalmist talks to himself too. And using the arrow to point from the "turmoil" to "within me" helps emphasize how much our lack of hope and faith affects our inner physical and mental well-being.

By lettering HOPE bold and beautiful, our eyes are turned from the inward struggle and directed by the arrow to the only One in whom true hope can be found. This leads us right into a banner declaring, "I shall again..." which speaks of the God of second chances, who never holds our wavering faith against us. Our focus turns from us to our God and our salvation, and our hearts are filled with praise.

As we've walked through this verse together, I hope you've been encouraged to try your hand at lettering a verse of your own, playing with different letter styles and sizes to express how God is speaking to you personally through it.

◉ Discover hand-lettering tutorials.

Karla

Chapter 7

Psalm 71: Continual Hope

In the midst of turmoil, how do we pray for God's help in a way that finds continual hope?

Day 1

Introducing Psalm 71

I prayed that Clay's MRI would show that whatever was causing my husband's lower back pain wouldn't be serious. It wasn't hard to hope for that, because the orthopedic surgeon said the chances of the cause being serious were slim.

But the MRI showed a tumor.

I prayed the tumor would be benign. Again, it wasn't hard to hope for that, because the oncologist said the chances of the tumor being malignant were extremely small.

But the lab diagnosed a rare form of bone cancer.

The oncologist said hospital labs sometimes misdiagnose rare cancers because they see them so seldom, so he wanted to see the slides himself before he decided how to proceed.

When I hung up the phone, I searched the Internet for information on the lab's diagnosis. The first link I found confirmed it was rare, all right—and 100 percent fatal within two years. Panic hit me like ice water and I could hear my heart pounding in my ears. I closed my computer and walked away.

I prayed the lab was wrong. But it was hard to hope for that. I didn't tell Clay what I'd seen.

Over the days that followed, worries whirled through my mind. Would Clay live? If not, how would I manage without him? If so, would he be disabled? Even if the lab were wrong, would surgery and recovery cost him the new job he was to start the next week? How would we manage financially?

My prayers jumbled into each other as I prayed over one anxious "what-if" to the point of reaching peace, only to have the "what-if-not" start the whirling again.

I prayed the lab was wrong. But it was hard to hope for that.

Psalm 71

Stanza I

1 In you, O LORD, do I take refuge;
       let me never be put to shame!

2 In your righteousness deliver me and rescue me;
       incline your ear to me, and save me!

3 Be to me a rock of refuge,
       to which I may continually come;
   you have given the command to save me,
       for you are my rock and my fortress.

4 Rescue me, O my God, from the hand of the wicked,
       from the grasp of the unjust and cruel man.

Stanza II

5 For you, O Lord, are my hope,
       my trust, O LORD, from my youth.

6 Upon you I have leaned from before my birth;
       you are he who took me from my mother's womb.
   My praise is continually of you.

7 I have been as a portent to many,
       but you are my strong refuge.

8 My mouth is filled with your praise,
       and with your glory all the day.

Stanza III

9 Do not cast me off in the time of old age;
       forsake me not when my strength is spent.

10 For my enemies speak concerning me;
       those who watch for my life consult together

11 and say, "God has forsaken him;
       pursue and seize him,
       for there is none to deliver him."

12 O God, be not far from me;
       O my God, make haste to help me!

13 May my accusers be put to shame and consumed;
       with scorn and disgrace may they be covered
       who seek my hurt.

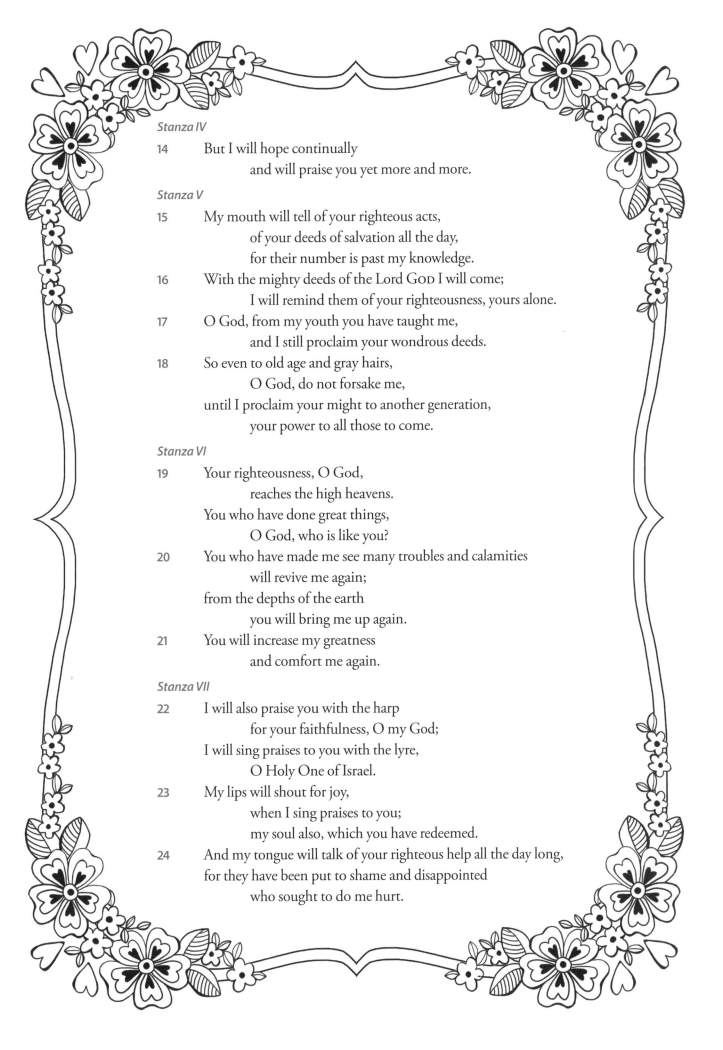

Stanza IV

14   But I will hope continually
           and will praise you yet more and more.

Stanza V

15   My mouth will tell of your righteous acts,
           of your deeds of salvation all the day,
           for their number is past my knowledge.

16   With the mighty deeds of the Lord GOD I will come;
           I will remind them of your righteousness, yours alone.

17   O God, from my youth you have taught me,
           and I still proclaim your wondrous deeds.

18   So even to old age and gray hairs,
           O God, do not forsake me,
    until I proclaim your might to another generation,
           your power to all those to come.

Stanza VI

19   Your righteousness, O God,
           reaches the high heavens.
    You who have done great things,
           O God, who is like you?

20   You who have made me see many troubles and calamities
           will revive me again;
    from the depths of the earth
           you will bring me up again.

21   You will increase my greatness
           and comfort me again.

Stanza VII

22   I will also praise you with the harp
           for your faithfulness, O my God;
    I will sing praises to you with the lyre,
           O Holy One of Israel.

23   My lips will shout for joy,
            when I sing praises to you;
           my soul also, which you have redeemed.

24   And my tongue will talk of your righteous help all the day long,
    for they have been put to shame and disappointed
           who sought to do me hurt.

The Little Details
Line Balance

In the New International Version, the number of lines within Psalm 71's stanzas are balanced on either side of the central line: 5-4-5-1-5-4-5.

I needed to pray a different way—a way that stopped trying to address all the possible tomorrows, a way that found hope bigger than human assurances.

The psalm we look at today shows us just that. It shows us how to pray with increasing and continual hope when trouble strikes: when we're out of work for months and the bank threatens foreclosure; when a coworker who didn't get the promotion we received slanders us and is believed; when a spouse's affection wanders; when our drug-addicted son refuses treatment.

Psalm 71 is a **lament** (a prayer about things gone wrong—a "prayer request" psalm) that we began looking at in the last chapter. It's a psalm written in old age by one who has walked with God from youth. Even in the advanced years of a godly person, events still occur that call for crying out for God's help. We will see how someone with many years of trusting God strengthens his faith in prayer.

We'll find the answer to this question: *When we're in the midst of turmoil, how do we pray for God's help in a way that results in continual hope?*

Psalm 71 is longer than the psalms in previous chapters, and so the daily lessons are a little longer too. But this psalm is worth it. Pray that God will speak to you through his Word, bring to mind any difficult situation you find yourself in, and then read Psalm 71.[1]

Initial Thoughts

1. What stands out to you from your initial reading of this psalm?

The Big Picture

You might have noticed our psalmist repeats words and themes quite a bit. Some of the repetitions link together the stanzas an equal distance from the center:

Repetitions				Stanza
A Let me never be put to shame, but in your righteousness deliver me				I
	B You took me from my mother's womb			II
		C Do not cast off or forsake me in old age		III
			D I will hope continually and praise more	IV
		C′ Do not forsake me even to old age		V
	B′ You will bring me up from earth's depths			VI
A′ My enemies have been put to shame with your righteous help				VII

Do you recognize this ABCDC'B'A' structure? It's a **chiasm** (KEY-azm). We've seen chiasms within lines—now we see an entire psalm arranged in a chiasm. In chiastic psalms, the theme is in the center.

2. What is Psalm 71's theme (verse 14)?

As we look into this psalm, we will see how the psalmist prayed so as to hope continually and praise more and more. He'll be our prayer mentor, so let's find out a little more about him.

The Psalmist

The psalm has no inscription, so we don't know who the author is. But the psalm itself tells us much about him.

3. (a) Besides writing psalms, what talents does he have (Psalm 71:22)? (b) When did he begin his relationship with God (verse 6)? (c) When did he begin relying on God (verse 5)? (d) Who was his teacher since childhood (verse 17)? (e) How old is he now (verse 9)? (f) What kind of life has he had (verse 20)?

Our psalmist is a gray-haired prayer warrior, poet, and musician. From childhood he has walked with God and learned from him. He's mature enough to have wisdom. He's met many troubles before, and he knows how to pray for help with hope and praise. He's experienced. He's a worthy mentor.

4. 🎵 What most interests you about the psalmist as a mentor? Why?

A Look Outward Sees Trouble

Now let's take a look at his current bind.

The Little Details
Who Wrote It?

Psalm 71 lacks an inscription, so we don't know who wrote it. We call such psalms **orphan psalms**.

Many think David wrote it because of its similarity to some of his other psalms and because the short psalm preceding it may be its introduction, in which case Psalm 70's inscription "Of David" applies to Psalm 71 as well. (Many of the untitled psalms are actually continuations of the preceding psalm.)

Others point out that some of the words used in this psalm may not have been common until the time of the exile, and suggest Jeremiah as a possible author.

Our psalmist is a gray-haired prayer warrior, poet, and musician.

5. (a) How does the psalmist describe the people with whom he's in conflict (Psalm 71:4)? (b) What happened to cause the psalmist to pray (verse 10)? (c) In those days, even those who didn't follow God often believed he existed. What do they say God has done (verse 11)? (d) How does the psalmist describe them in verse 13? (e) What do they seek to do (verse 24)?

The psalmist finds himself attacked by enemies who wish to kill him and who say God has forsaken him. He asks that God not shame him by forsaking him, as his enemies claim God has done.

Are you surprised to read words like "do not forsake me" and "do not be far from me" coming from a man of God? Have you ever cried, "God, where are you?" I have, and it's encouraging that God included in the Psalms an example of someone facing those same feelings even after years of walking with him.

The psalmist, however, does not continue to question God's care. He prays in a way that strengthens faith as he reaches to find God. Although the circumstances we face presently may not be life-threatening, we can use this prayer as an example to strengthen our own faith in any circumstance.

6. The psalmist speaks of enemies. (a) According to Ephesians 6:11-12, against whose schemes must we stand? (b) Against whom do we wrestle?

These spiritual enemies accuse, deceive, dishearten, and tempt. They strive to weaken our faith, stop us from maturing in Christ, and keep us from fulfilling the ministry God calls us to do. When we face difficulties, it's important to remember that we're wrestling with spiritual enemies.

7. These aren't the only "enemies" that accuse, deceive, dishearten, or tempt. Check the boxes of all you've faced:
   ☐ Life-threatening circumstances
   ☐ Someone's jealousy
   ☐ Unfriendly competitors
   ☐ Someone who hates or dislikes you
   ☐ Someone seeking revenge
   ☐ Accusers
   ☐ Slanderers and gossipers
   ☐ Con artists
   ☐ Thieves

We can use this prayer as an example to strengthen our own faith in any circumstance.

- ☐ Manipulators out for their own gain at your expense
- ☐ Liars
- ☐ Difficulties that threaten faith
- ☐ Tragedy
- ☐ Loss
- ☐ Other:

What does our psalmist do when he learns his enemies seek to destroy him? He pens a prayer. And not just any prayer. It's a prayer that builds hope even as it reaches to find God. It's a prayer that shows us how to strengthen our hope in troubled times.

Experiencing Psalm 71 Creatively

Begin thinking of other ways to interact with Psalm 71. For inspiration, review Chapter 1, Day 1. Here are some ideas specific to this chapter's psalm:

- Find a tall rock to display that will remind you that God is your rock of refuge.

- Tell a younger person about something God has done in your life.

- Write a letter to an older person whose life has shown you God, explaining how he or she has been to you what the psalmist wants to be to younger people. Accompany the letter with a sweet treat.

Hope Alive

You and I want to be women who faithfully follow Jesus into our silver-haired days so we can each be a beacon of hope and help to the generations that follow. But what do we do when fears threaten to overtake our faith? The psalmist illuminates the way through these times.

> O God, from my youth you have taught me,
>   and I still proclaim your wondrous deeds.
> So even to old age and gray hairs,
>   O God, do not forsake me,
> until I proclaim your might to another generation,
>   your power to all those to come (Psalm 71:17-18).

In simple terms, the psalmist calls us to:

> Look back so we can move forward.
> Look up so we don't become downcast.

In my book *Becoming a Brave New Woman*, I tell the story of a time when Bill and I faced a move to the inner city so he could attend seminary. I was so depressed about it that Bill pleaded with me to talk with a mentor. I called Barbara, the mother of one of our close friends. She had experienced tragedies and obstacles, yet she had a zest for life I knew was empowered by her love for God and her hope in his Word.

This young, fearful newlywed sat at this seasoned saint's kitchen table as she recounted to me the faithfulness of God. She took out her worn Bible and flipped from favorite verse to favorite verse, telling me stories of God's faithfulness. That day I created a plan of faithfulness: (1) Get to know God by digging deeper into his Word and marking passages as I learn; (2) get a journal and keep track of God's faithfulness to me so I can share it with others; and (3) get in the habit of recalling God's character and faithfulness so it's natural to turn to him.

Now I am the gray-haired grandmother. (Well, at least under the blond highlights I pay for!) And in my legacy-living days, I've added more ways to meditate on God's goodness and share it. I place myself in Bible explorations with leaders who challenge me like Jean has in this study of Psalms. I have markers to make notes alongside verses as God comforts and guides me. I display favorite verses in creative ways: I keep a "miracle scrapbook"; I hang photos and paintings of special passages; I sketch and I write prose and poetry capturing names and traits of God. And I bring the act of praise into natural rhythms of my life. For example, when I swim each week, I pray through the attributes of God, A to Z, recounting his character. This gives me confidence. And before I get out of my cozy bed to face this often harsh world, I recall the names of God. My friend, Jill Savage, founder of Hearts at Home, says, "Look at the mountain-mover, not the mountain."

No matter what we face, Psalm 71 inspires us to express a legacy of joy and hope:

> My lips will shout for joy,
>> when I sing praises to you;
>> my soul also, which you have redeemed.
> And my tongue will talk of your righteous help all the day long
>> (Psalm 71: 23-24).

Recalling God's help and comfort builds my hope, and I pray it builds the faith of my kids and grandkids, my friends, my readers, and even strangers. You and I can join the psalmist in passing the baton of faith from generation to generation. Let's stay true, creative, and faithful!

⊙ Discover attributes of God to pray.

Pam

The Little Details

Rocks of Refuge

- Samson took refuge from the Philistines in a cleft of the rock of Etam (Judges 15:8).

- Six hundred Benjamites hid from pursuers for four months in the rock of Rimmon (Judges 20:47).

- David took refuge from Saul in a mountainous rock he later named the Rock of Escape (1 Samuel 23:25-28).

- David built a stronghold in the cave of Adullam, which was in a rock where he encamped when fighting the Philistines (1 Chronicles 11:15).

Only One has the power and faithfulness to be always worthy of trust.

Day 2

Hope from God's Character and Deeds

Today we're reading the prayer of someone who knew God well, and his prayer shows it. He looked outward and saw trouble, so now he lifts his eyes to God and prays.

Look Up to Find Hope in God's Character

He begins his prayer by calling on what he knows about God.

> **8.** Read the first stanza (Psalm 71:1-4). List the ways the psalmist describes God.

The psalmist's requests are grounded in what he knew about God.

God Is Our Rock

Pursued by enemies, the psalmist might have trusted in his own power and authority, in the faithfulness of the people around him, or in his wealth. He might have fled to a mountain pocked with caves and split with clefts too numerous for pursuers to search—a rock of refuge. He could have taken refuge in a mighty fortress with tall towers and walls high enough and strong enough to resist armies.

But none of these are what the psalmist seeks. All of these can fail. Only One has the power and faithfulness to be always worthy of trust.

The psalmist calls God his "refuge," "rock of refuge," "rock," and "fortress." The Old and New Testaments often refer to God as a rock. The term carries the meaning of a strong place of defense. In many psalms, *rock* is combined with *fortress*, strengthening the idea of a safe place in times of trouble.

> **9.** Because he has taken refuge in the Lord, what does the psalmist request (71:1)?

Allen P. Ross, professor of divinity at Beeson Divinity School, says this about psalms that ask for the psalmist never to be put to shame and for enemies to be put to shame instead:

> The use of "put to shame, be ashamed"...refers to the disgrace and humiliation of having everything that was once honored and valued overthrown and brought to nothing; and that would include the psalmist's faith, for if God allowed the enemies to destroy him, what he believed would be considered worthless in the eyes of his enemies. The prayer will be that the enemies be put to shame instead of him, that God would show their beliefs and actions to be false. [2]

God Is Righteous

The psalmist now asks God to act based on God's character.

10. (a) In Psalm 71:2, on what attribute of God does the psalmist call? (b) What four requests does he make based on this attribute?

11. How does he describe his attackers (71:4)?

The psalmist asks God to act in his righteousness, for the men who pursue him are wicked, unjust, and cruel. When someone attacks us wrongly, we can ask God to act in his righteousness to bring justice in the situation, entrusting ourselves to him who judges justly (1 Peter 2:19-23).

When we call on God's attributes in our prayers, we are not trying to talk God into answering us; instead, we are reminding ourselves of why God would want to answer. In so doing, we find hope in who God is.

What are ways we can call on God's attributes? The unemployed can find hope in God as Provider. The victim of lies can remember Jesus is Truth. The wronged spouse can dwell on God's faithfulness. Discouraged parents can know God loves their children even more than they do. The criticized can dwell on God's patience and acceptance. The rejected can embrace God as the perfect Father who will never abandon them.

12. 🎵 On the My Psalm page at the end of this chapter, write your name next to "A Psalm of." Below that write a prayer that begins with a statement of trust and that requests help based on God's attributes.

Look Back to Find Hope in God's Past Help

The psalmist has looked up to God and prayed according to God's attributes. Now his gaze shifts and he looks to his past to recall how God has come through for him before.

The Little Details
Song of Moses

How did the psalmist know God's character? He may have learned about God from the Song of Moses. God gave this song to Moses and commanded him to teach all Israelites to sing it and to teach it to their descendants (Deuteronomy 31:19-21). The song taught them about God and his relationship to Israel:

> The Rock! His work is perfect, / For all His ways are just; / A God of faithfulness and without injustice, / Righteous and upright is He (Deuteronomy 32:4 NASB).

When we call on God's attributes in our prayers, we are not trying to talk God into answering us; instead, we are reminding ourselves of why God would want to answer.

The Little Details

Portents

Many prophets' lives were portents—signs of things to come, either as assurance or warning.

For instance, the prophet Isaiah said his children and he were portents: one child's birth and first words were a sign to a wayward king of the coming fall of his enemies; and for three years Isaiah walked barefoot and stripped as a portent of what would happen to Egypt (Isaiah 8:18; 20:3).

God often asked the prophet Jeremiah to act as a portent, such as when he bought a field that would soon be lost as a sign that the Jews would be restored to the land after their exile.

At times portents were of something momentous that would happen many generations in the future. Abraham's offering of his son Isaac portended the Father's offering of his Son Jesus, and King David's earthly rule portended Jesus' eternal rule.

- -

Few things build hope more than remembering God's faithfulness to us in the past.

- -

13. Read Psalm 71's second stanza (verses 5-8). (a) What two things has the Lord been to the psalmist (verse 5)? (b) For how long has this been the case? (c) Even before he learned to make God his hope and trust, he leaned on God ("from birth," most translations say). Who delivered him from his mother's womb (verse 6)? (d) What resulted from making the Lord his hope and trust (verse 6c)?

The psalmist recalls how he had made God his hope and trust in the past, and how that had resulted in continually praising God. Recalling the ways God previously has rewarded our hope and trust causes our hope to soar because it encourages us to expect the same result now.

In the next verse, the psalmist says he has been "as a portent to many." A *portent* is a sign foreshadowing something to come. When we set our hope in God and people see how he preserves us, our lives become signs to others of what God can do for them.

14. (a) Many considered the psalmist's life a marvelous sign of what to expect from God. What is God to him (71:7)? (b) What fills the psalmist's mouth as he remembers God's help throughout his life (71:8)?

As the psalmist reviews his life, he remembers that God has always been a strong refuge to him. His faith begins to soar and his heart erupts in praise.

Few things build hope more than remembering God's faithfulness to us in the past. So important is it that God told the Israelites to set up "stones of remembrance" and celebrate holidays ("holy days") so they would not forget his hand in their lives (Joshua 4:1-9; Leviticus 23:41-43).

15. 🎵 What are three wonders in your own life that assure you God is your refuge?

Hold on to these! They will help you find hope in troubled times.

16. 🎵 Turn to the My Psalm page. Skip a line and write a prayer of thanksgiving for these wonders in your life.

Hope for Today

I once thought prayers had to sound spiritual; that is, I had to claim things I didn't really feel but thought I should feel. For instance, with heart pounding and palms sweating I would pray, "I'm not afraid." Or I'd say, "I'm totally fine about what's happened," when I hadn't considered if I truly was fine. I was supposed to be fine, so of course I was fine.

I resisted looking deep within me, partly in case I should find something I thought shouldn't be there, and partly because I thought saying things were fine would in some way make it so.

But this wasn't honest prayer.

There came a day when, in the midst of grieving a loss, it struck me that God already knew everything in my heart. I was the only one between us who wasn't looking inside me. And if I didn't look, then how would I know what really needed prayer?

My prayers changed that day. I began looking deep within to expose my true feelings, weaknesses, and desires to both myself and to God. I began praying honestly. God didn't forsake me over what we saw; after all, he already knew. Instead, we grew closer and I saw him begin to strengthen the weak areas formerly hidden from me.

On Day 2 we looked at two prayer elements that strengthen faith: praying according to God's character and praying in remembrance of God's past help. Today we'll look at two more. The first is looking inward to pray honestly.

Look Inward to Pray

Take a look at Psalm 71's third stanza.

> **17.** Read Psalm 71:9-13. What strikes you most?

> **18.** (a) What weaknesses does the psalmist have (Psalm 71:9)? (b) How does he pray about these weaknesses?

Are you surprised this man of faith isn't praying, "I know you'll never cast me off, and I know you'll never forsake me, even though I'm old and weak"?

Instead, he looks within to see what his thoughts and emotions are telling him. He realizes he's not all he used to be. The younger fellows are doing what he used to do. Perhaps people don't value him as much. A fear creeps in: *Does God still value me when I can't do what I used to do for him?*

God already knew everything in my heart. I was the only one between us who wasn't looking inside me.

The Little Details
What to Avoid in Prayer

We should avoid **grumbling** like the Israelites grumbled when they tired of eating manna in the desert and forgot the manna was God's gift (1 Corinthians 10:10).

We shouldn't **test God** by questioning his ability to meet human demands (Psalm 78:18-19; 1 Corinthians 10:9).

Neither should we **accuse God of sin**, as the prophet Jeremiah discovered when he asked God if he were trying to deceive him by allowing painful persecution. God told him if he repented and spoke "worthy words" rather than "worthless words," he could continue to be God's mouthpiece. God then reassured Jeremiah that he was strengthening him to make him able to withstand these attacks (Jeremiah 15:18-20).

If you catch yourself erring in any of these ways, simply confess it, turn from it, receive forgiveness, and continue your prayer rightly. God will strengthen you as he strengthened Jeremiah.

- -

How can God show me I don't need to fear something if I won't admit I do fear it?

- -

19. What else may fuel this fear (71:10-11)?

We don't know why his enemies conclude God's forsaken him. It could be a recent trouble or his fading strength. Whatever it is, when he heard his enemies' words, they didn't bounce off like fiery darts striking a bronze wall. They pierced.

The psalmist took the hurtful words to God.

20. What two requests does the psalmist make in verse 12?

The psalmist apparently cannot feel God's presence. But not sensing God's presence doesn't mean he's not there. God promises, "I will never leave you nor forsake you" (Hebrews 13:5).

Not sensing God's presence is part of tests of faith. How a child acts when her parents aren't present is a much better indicator of what the child is like than how she acts when she knows her parents are watching. Likewise, how we act when we can't feel God's presence is a better indicator of our faith than when his presence amazes us with his glory and majesty.

The psalmist brings his fears honestly to God. When prayers skirt around the real issue, we find no hope. But when we respectfully and without grumbling lay out before God everything we're feeling, no matter how unspiritual it sounds, we find hope in God's acceptance of us as we truly are. Then he can minister to our true area of need. After all, how can God show me I don't need to fear something if I won't admit I do fear it?

Although sinful attitudes can produce sinful prayers, honesty springing from a faithful heart won't be sinful (see sidebar).

The psalmist lays out not only his fears before God, but also what he desires God to do.

21. What does the psalmist want (Psalm 71:13)?

The psalmist prays that what his enemies are doing to him would fall back on them. They claimed God had forsaken him: Let him not be ashamed, but rather let them be so when they see God is surely still with him.

This prayer might seem a little odd, and a little background will help. The psalmists lived under the Mosaic Law, which said this in Deuteronomy 19:19-21:

You shall do to him as he had meant to do to his brother. So you shall purge the evil from your midst. And the rest shall hear and fear, and shall never again commit any such evil among you. Your eye shall not pity. It shall be life for life, eye for eye, tooth for tooth, hand for hand, foot for foot.

That's why psalmists sometimes prayed for others to be paid back tit for tat. The law's intent was both to deter wrongdoing and to prevent angry avengers from over-punishing.

When Jesus came, he taught us to be even more gracious than the Law allowed: "But if anyone slaps you on the right cheek, turn to him the other also" (Matthew 5:39).

> **22.** (a) Underline what Romans 12:17-19 below says about revenge. (b) Circle who will repay evil.
>
> Repay no one evil for evil, but give thought to do what is honorable in the sight of all. If possible, so far as it depends on you, live peaceably with all. Beloved, never avenge yourselves, but leave it to the wrath of God, for it is written, "Vengeance is mine, I will repay, says the Lord."

> **23.** In Luke 6:27-28 below, Jesus tells us how we should treat those who intentionally wrong us. Underline and number the four actions we should take.
>
> I say to you who hear, Love your enemies, do good to those who hate you, bless those who curse you, pray for those who abuse you.

How do we pray for those who maliciously hurt us, as happened to the psalmist?

Psalm 71:13 says, "May my accusers be put to shame and consumed." At first glance, that may not seem to jibe with the fuller revelation Jesus brought. However, having the false beliefs that led to their sinful actions put to shame might lead them to repent. At its mildest, shame is that tugging of our conscience when we've done something wrong. It's the conviction of the Holy Spirit. Its purpose is to bring us to repentance.

When we're wronged by unbelievers, we can pray for the Holy Spirit to convict them of sin and draw the wrongdoers to repentance and salvation. If they repent, the blood of Jesus will pay for their sin and he will have already borne their "scorn and disgrace" (Psalm 71:13). If they don't repent, they will be "consumed" at the judgment, as the psalmist prayed.

When we're wronged by a believer, Jesus says to "go and tell him his fault, between you and him alone" (Matthew 18:15). Before we go to our brother or sister in Christ, we can pray for the Holy Spirit to convict of sin and draw the believer to repentance so he or she can grow. That's what we want for ourselves when we've hurt others, isn't it?

These prayers for justice remind us that God is both merciful and just. Justice will be done, whether through the cross or the consuming judgment.

Whether or not our troubles involve being wronged by another, we can pray honestly. Do our troubles make us dread others' judgments? Do they seed doubts over God's love and forgiveness? Do they raise questions about our worth? We can lay everything out in prayer.

How can God show me I don't need to fear something if I won't admit I do fear it?

24. ♪ Turn to the My Psalm page. Skip a line and write a prayer honestly expressing your fears and desires.

Look Up in Continual Hope

The psalmist has looked outward and seen trouble, upward to find hope in God's character, back to find hope in God's prior saving acts, and inward to pray honestly. Now he comes to his prayer's focus.

25. Read Psalm 71's fourth stanza (verse 14). What are the two things the psalmist commits to doing?

This is the prayer's theme. All the preceding lines have led up to this line, and those yet to come flow from it. The psalmist has set his will to do two things around which the entire psalm revolves.

Hope Continually

We have a hope God has given us by his great promises. It's not something we see yet, for then it would not be hope but rather hope realized.[3] Yet it is a certain hope, one we can rest in during times of trouble, one that will not disappoint.[4]

Praise God More and More

Because the psalmist has hope, he will praise God yet more and more. He now is certain God will do good by him, and so he praises freely.

This is not the same as putting on a happy face and pretending all is fine. The psalmist sees his troubles clearly, but finds hope in what he knows about God. He commits to hoping in God continually and to praising God as he sees that hope fulfilled.

26. ♪ On the My Psalm page, write a commitment to hope in God and praise him for how he'll answer your prayer. Use Psalm 71:14 if you want.

Day 4

Hope for Tomorrow

One of the strangely disconcerting things to me during my husband's bout with cancer was the feeling of losing purpose. Clay had just finished his doctorate and was applying for jobs at churches and universities. We expected that he would continue to work in ministry in one of those two forums, and that I would help in whatever he did, work part-time programming, and serve in women's ministry at our church.

Now all that seemed jeopardized by two real possibilities: he might not live long enough to fulfill any of these dreams or (if he did) disabilities might hinder his employment.

A strange thought floated into my head: *I thought God had a greater purpose for us than this.*

I felt unvalued, but was it true? No! I knew God valued us both: He loved us and had saved us. I also knew he is the one who decides what our ministries and purposes will be on earth. Whether a ministry seemed valuable in my eyes didn't necessarily reflect how valuable it was in God's eyes, and I couldn't know his reasons for this difficulty. His purposes are often unseen.

I knew, however, that all Christians have one purpose in common: living so as to glorify God. I could respond daily with faith in God's goodness and with trust that his plans for us are ultimately for good. Whatever happened, I would be able to testify to God's goodness.

That's what the psalmist speaks of next: Whatever happens, he will fulfill his purpose of testifying.

Look Ahead to Life's Purpose

In the first half of the psalm, the psalmist looks at his circumstances in the light of how they would immediately affect him. From that view, he prays, "Save me!" The way he asked strengthened his hope. In the second half of the psalm, his prayers flow from that hope.

> **27.** Read Psalm 71's fifth stanza (verses 15-18), paying attention to the actions the psalmist plans to take. What's the gist of what he wants to do?

This prayer reflects five foundational understandings.

God's Plan Is Bigger Than What We Can See

> **28.** (a) What is the psalmist going to do (Psalm 71:15a-b)? (b) How often does God perform saving deeds? (c) What is beyond the psalmist's knowledge (15c)?

> Whether a ministry seemed valuable in my eyes didn't necessarily reflect how valuable it was in God's eyes.

On earth we cannot know all the ways God has orchestrated good for us, all the evils he's stopped, or all the working of good from bad that he's woven into the unfinished tapestry of our lives. We cannot know today what hidden workings God already has begun in our current struggles.

When troubles loom, remembering this brings perspective. When thoughts spawned from the whispers of spiritual enemies taunt us that God has forsaken us, we can tell of God's righteous acts and deeds of salvation, remembering there are more than we know.

> **29.** 🌗 (a) What are some of the righteous acts and deeds of salvation God has worked in your life? (b) Describe a time God brought an unexpected good from a difficulty.

The psalmist isn't looking at his troubles at this moment. He's looking at how he can fulfill his purpose on earth: He can proclaim the wonderful acts of God.

God has a purpose bigger than any of us individually. It includes a plan for the entire world, in all generations. Sometimes the accomplishment of the fullness of that plan means allowing his beloved children to suffer. This was true of his Son, Jesus, and it is true of those who follow his Son.

Years later, the apostle Paul sat in a sweltering Roman prison for preaching about Jesus as the Messiah, for which he faced the death penalty. He wrote these words (Philippians 1:20-22) explaining how he found purpose amid hardship:

> It is my eager expectation and hope that I will not be at all ashamed, but that with full courage now as always Christ will be honored in my body, whether by life or by death. For to me to live is Christ, and to die is gain. If I am to live in the flesh, that means fruitful labor for me. Yet which I shall choose I cannot tell.

To die meant going to be with God; to live meant God had fruitful labor for him on earth.

God does not leave us to fulfill his purpose for us on our own, however. He gives us his strength. This is the next foundation on which the psalmist's prayer rests.

God Gives Us His Strength

> **30.** (a) When he goes to speak to others, with what will he come (Psalm 71:16)? (b) Compare this verse with verse 9. Who has strength and who lacks it?

The psalmist isn't trying to impress others with his own strength, but with God's mighty deeds.

One reason we have weaknesses is "to show that the surpassing power belongs to God and not to us" (2 Corinthians 4:7). Although physically the psalmist's strength is failing as he ages, yet he can go forth in the strength of the Lord. God gives him the strength he needs to accomplish God's purposes: "I can do all things through him who strengthens me" (Philippians 4:13). Where he is weak, God's might will all the more display.

Knowing God's plan is bigger than he can see and that God strengthens him to fulfill it allows the psalmist to react to accusations with another foundational understanding: God's righteousness is more important than our own.

God's Righteousness Counts More Than Ours

The psalmist again speaks of the attribute of God in which he finds hope: his righteousness.

31. Of whose righteousness will he remind people (71:16)?

In verse 13, the psalmist calls his enemies "accusers." When accused, we naturally want to proclaim to everyone how unjust the accusations are and how rightly we've acted. Yet the psalmist makes no mention of this. He says he'll remind everyone only of God's righteousness.

Perhaps in his old age he's so aware of God's righteousness compared to his own that he's unconcerned with defending himself. Perhaps he's resting in knowing God's righteousness will prevail. Perhaps he realizes his own righteousness comes from God through faith, even though he does not yet know the name of the One whose sacrifice brings that righteousness.

Later the apostle Paul summed up righteousness in this way (Philippians 3:8-9):

> I have suffered the loss of all things and count them as rubbish, in order that I may gain Christ and be found in him, not having a righteousness of my own that comes from the law, but that which comes through faith in Christ, the righteousness from God that depends on faith.

Whatever the psalmist's reason, his goal is to proclaim God's righteousness, not his own.

The psalmist has another foundational truth garnered from having walked with God closely from childhood: God continually teaches us.

God Teaches Us Continually

32. (a) In Psalm 71:17, what has God done since his youth? (b) What does the psalmist proclaim?

That God teaches us continually is one of his wondrous deeds. In fact, he teaches us through hardships (Romans 5:3-5):

> We rejoice in our sufferings, knowing that suffering produces endurance, and endurance produces character, and character produces hope, and hope does not put us to shame, because God's love has been poured into our hearts through the Holy Spirit who has been given to us.

The psalmist has faced many troubles and calamities (verse 20), and God has taught him much through them. The current troubles will be no different. His enemies may see his current troubles as a sign that God has forsaken him (verse 11), but the psalmist knows God allows difficulties in the lives of his beloved and uses them to teach.

33. ♪ (a) What have the difficulties in your life taught you about God? (b) How does remembering how we've grown spiritually through past troubles bring hope in current troubles?

Now the psalmist sees his purpose.

We Have Purpose Even When We're Weak

That he has purpose even in old age is a truth the psalmist now sees.

34. (a) What does the psalmist again ask (71:18)? (b) The psalmist's requests earlier were about his own needs (verse 9). About whose needs is he concerned now?

Before, the psalmist feared God might forsake him because he lacked usefulness since his strength was gone. Now he not only sees God's might and power as being what he needs in his weakness, but he knows that even if God does not enlighten him as to the reasons for his current troubles, he can accomplish one thing of eternal worth: He can tell others of God's wondrous works, strength, and power. Faith that stands firm through the fiery tests of hell is faith that gives witness to all.

35. ♪ How have your past troubles enabled you to help someone?

36. This stanza's theme ties back to the third stanza. How does the psalmist's testimony about God's actions dispute what his enemies claimed about God in verse 11?

While Clay and I awaited his surgery for cancer, we did not fully know how God would use this difficulty. But we did know this: When we go through hardships trusting God, our testimony of God's goodness is strengthened.

Each day I prayed for the grace to meet that day's challenges with faith, and I committed to faithfulness no matter what, because I remembered my purpose: to proclaim God with my life and words.

When we're out of work for months but still depend on God as Provider and give thanks for every bit of help that arrives, we fulfill our purpose. When we stand firm in the face of malicious slander and trust in the God who will one day make all truth known, we fulfill our purpose. When we grieve abandonment by people, but turn to the God who will never abandon us, we fulfill our purpose. When we turn our children over to God and trust that he knows best how to reach them, we fulfill our purpose.

37. 🌙 How can you fulfill God's purpose for you in your current difficulties?

38. 🎵 Turn to the My Psalm page. Skip a line and write a prayer of faith, expressing trust in what you cannot see and reliance on God's strength to fulfill his purpose for you.

When we go through hardships trusting God, our testimony of God's goodness is strengthened.

An Eternal View

In this chapter, we saw our psalmist strengthen his faith in prayer. Today, we see the results: a soaring faith that looks forward to eternity, and then back to today from an eternal viewpoint.

Look to Eternity

In the sixth stanza, the psalmist proclaims three truths about God that we, too, can proclaim.

He Proclaims God's Righteousness

> **39.** Read Psalm 71's sixth stanza (verses 19-21). (a) What does the psalmist proclaim about God in 19a-b? (b) What praises fill the psalmist's mouth in 19c-d?

In stanza I, the psalmist found hope in God's righteousness. Now he praises God for that righteousness. In stanza II, he found hope in God's past help. Here he praises God's deeds.

He Proclaims God's Final Rescue from Troubles

By looking beyond life on earth to eternity, the psalmist sees God's final rescue from this life's troubles.

> **40.** (a) What does looking back at his past troubles assure the psalmist God will do for him (verse 20a-b)? (b) The word *again* tells us God has revived (or kept alive) the psalmist through past troubles. From where will God take him at the end of physical life (20c-d)?

The phrase "troubles and calamities" is parallel to "depths of the earth," emphasizing that troubles are on earth, not in the afterlife. That God has revived him from troubles before explains how he has been a portent to others (stanza II). Just as God took him from his mother's womb to begin his earthly life (stanza II), so God will take him from the earth's depths to eternal life.

He Proclaims the Glory and Comfort to Come

The psalmist now proclaims what will come in eternity.

By looking beyond life on earth to eternity, the psalmist sees God's final rescue from this life's troubles.

41. What will God do for the psalmist when he enters his new life (Psalm 71:21)?

In this stanza, the psalmist's view is no longer limited to temporal causes and effects. He sees that God's righteousness is high (verse 19)—higher, in fact, than this life. Although this life has been filled with severe troubles, God has always revived him. Even if he should now die, God will revive him again and bring him to new life.

Hoping for that which will come is key to getting through the difficulties of this life. Although all will be lost here, we have hope in a glorious future.[5]

42. In 1 Peter 1:13 below, underline where our hope should rest.

> Preparing your minds for action, and being sober-minded, set your hope fully on the grace that will be brought to you at the revelation of Jesus Christ.

The psalmist did not expect all God's promises to be fulfilled in this life, but he looked forward to the new life to come. In that new life, two things await.

In eternity God will increase his greatness. This is the opposite of what his enemies sought for him. This increased greatness awaits all who remain faithful to God through hard times. Even if the enemies should overtake him now, they cannot put him to shame in the end, for all who remain faithful to God receive at the resurrection not shame, but glory.

Indeed, the glory we'll receive then will make our current troubles seem slight. Paul writes in 2 Corinthians 4:16-18:

> We do not lose heart. Though our outer self is wasting away, our inner self is being renewed day by day. For this light momentary affliction is preparing for us an eternal weight of glory beyond all comparison, as we look not to the things that are seen but to the things that are unseen. For the things that are seen are transient, but the things that are unseen are eternal.

In eternity God will comfort him on every side. In the next life, false accusations will fade when God makes truth known and ends injustice. He'll give us strong and healthy new bodies. He'll destroy evil and all that causes sin. He'll wipe away the pain and sorrow of this life. He'll give us an eternal home in heaven that can never be lost. He'll reward our work, perseverance, and faithfulness. We will finally dwell with the God of perfect love, who will never forsake or abandon us.[6]

In comparison to the glory and comfort to come, the troubles of this life are light; and in comparison to an eternity of glory, temporal suffering is but momentary.

43. ♪ Turn to the My Psalm page. Review what you've written so far. Skip a line and write a prayer that looks to and proclaims the hope that is to come.

Hoping for that which will come is key to getting through the difficulties of this life.

Look from Eternity

In the last stanza, the psalmist looks from eternity's vantage point back at his earthly troubles and sees the final answer as already accomplished.

> **44.** Read Psalm 71's seventh stanza (verses 22-24). (a) For what two things will the psalmist praise God (22b and 23c)? (b) Of what will the psalmist talk (24a)? (c) How has God helped the psalmist (24b-c)?

This is the fifth mention of God's righteousness. The psalmist has gone from asking for help based on God's righteousness (verse 2), to finding purpose in proclaiming God's righteous acts (verses 15-16), to praising God over the greatness of his righteousness (verse 19), to proclaiming to others God's righteous help (verse 24).

In the final stanza, the psalmist's faith soars and he fills the poem's lines with words of praise. His eyes are opened to eternity, and from there he sees three things:

From Eternity He Sees God's Faithfulness

In the first line of the poem, the psalmist puts his trust in God, saying, "Let me never be put to shame." In the view from eternity, the psalmist sees his answer as accomplished.

From Eternity He Sees His Soul's Redemption

In the first stanzas of the psalm, the psalmist asks to be delivered from evil men who wish to take his life. In this last stanza, he sees his final deliverance in the redemption of his soul. He has grasped what Jesus would later teach in Matthew 10:28:

> Do not fear those who kill the body but cannot kill the soul. Rather fear him who can destroy both soul and body in hell.

Years later, a Son of David will suffer and die at the hands of wicked and evil men who despise and abhor him. Through his willingness to shed his blood, he will bring about the redemption the psalmist here foresees.

From Eternity He Sees Final Justice

God has promised a day of judgment when everything will be made right. For this, the psalmist's tongue cannot cease to talk of God's righteousness.

> **45.** ♪ Turn to the My Psalm page. Skip a line and write a prayer expressing (a) what you praise God for today; (b) what you want to tell others about God's help and redemption; and (c) what will be the eternal conclusion of your current circumstances.

The psalmist's eyes are opened to eternity, and from there he sees three things—God's faithfulness, his soul's redemption, and final justice.

Notice how the psalmist's view has traveled:

Before praying	He looks **outward** at his troubling external circumstances and turns to God in prayer
Stanza I	He looks **up** to God, putting his hope in him and petitioning him according to the attributes that God has made known about himself
Stanza II	He looks **back** to his past and finds hope in remembering God's past help
Stanza III	He looks **inward** to expose his fears and desires plainly before God, finding hope in God's acceptance
Stanza IV	He looks **up** again, in continual hope and praise
Stanza V	He looks **forward** in the hope of what purpose the rest of his life could contribute to the generation around him as well as to those to come
Stanza VI	He looks **further forward** to finding hope in the resurrection and the glory to come
Stanza VII	He looks **back** from the standpoint of eternity and sees his redemption and his enemies' condemnation as things accomplished and his hope fulfilled

The psalmist sees the big picture in which his circumstances are placed, and that strengthens his faith, bringing forth praise.

46. ♪ What elements of this psalm are most encouraging to you? Why?

The central theme of Psalm 71 is in verse 14: "But I will hope continually, and will praise you yet more and more." In these last two stanzas we see the psalmist's hope, and we see him fulfill his promise as his pen flows with more and more praise.

When we're in the midst of affliction, we don't know what good God intends to accomplish for us on earth. Sometimes we see some of the answers here; sometimes we wait until eternity to know the answers.

> When we're in the midst of affliction, we don't know what good God intends to accomplish for us on earth.

Clay and I saw parts of what good God intended through Clay's cancer. The first laboratory's diagnosis of Clay having a fatal, fast-growing cancer was wrong: His was a slower-growing, treatable cancer. He lost his teaching contract for only one class, and soon after another university hired him part-time to oversee online courses from home while he recovered. That led to a full-time teaching position there the following semester. His experience gives weight and authority to his class on why God allows evil.

It was part of God's purpose and plan to bring people to his heart and wisdom.

Worshiping Through Supplications

Prayer is one of the principal ways we worship God. Our prayer requests—supplications—are worship when our hearts open honestly and vulnerably before God as we address him as who he is and place hope in his promises. Our entreaties are worship when our souls spontaneously pour out gratitude and praise for God's gifts and help. Our pleas are worship when they look forward to the glory that is to come.

Worshiping with Laments

We worshiped with laments (psalms about things gone wrong) in the last chapter as prayers that intercede for others. In this chapter you'll worship with them as prayers for yourself.

Get alone with God so you can worship wholeheartedly.

Psalm 71

We prayed for others with Psalm 71 in the last chapter.

- *Optional:* If you'd like to worship with Psalm 71 again, this time praying for yourself, turn to Psalm 71 in your Bible and pray its words to God.

My Psalm

Make sure you're someplace quiet so you can really talk to God. The psalm you wrote is a personalized version of Psalm 71.

- Pray through your psalm slowly, aloud. When finished, record any answers or assurances you sense.

May praying the psalms become a regular part of your worship!

My Psalm ————————————————————————————————

A Psalm of:

Creative Connection

This chapter's verse, Psalm 71:14, inspired me to draw a girl with her hands lifted high and heavenward praising God—"yet more and more." That's the image that came to mind. But not everyone lifts their hands when they worship the Lord, do they? Some people worship on their knees and others don't. Still others worship in dance. And that's okay because God created us all to be unique individuals, and he gave us the capacity and desire to creatively worship and connect with him in a variety of ways, including with art.

God is the author of all creation. He formed us and gifted us with the ability to be creative—to be like him! He is the One who inspires the colors we choose and the mediums we use to express ourselves, whether we're seasoned artists or beginners, whether we're using colored pencils in a coloring book, acrylics to paint a masterpiece, or a pen to create a poem. Some people lean toward bright primary colors, while others find their joy in pastels. Some love loose and abstract, while others find pleasure in the tiny little details. And sometimes those leanings change with the seasons of life. That's all okay. The point is that God wants us to accept ourselves as he designed us and, at the same time, continue to grow as his children and as artists.

Be encouraged to creatively play, explore, and experiment with different color palettes, mediums, and art styles until you find that sweet spot in your heart that connects with God's. And as you color Psalm 71:14, I pray you will remember that God not only wants you to hope continually, but he also wants you to grow continually and choose to praise him more and more.

⊙ Discover plenty more creative inspiration.

Karla

Chapter 8

Psalms 30 and 146:
Hope Fulfilled

How should we respond to answered prayers?

Day 1

Introducing Psalms 30 and 146

When the lab diagnosed my husband's tumor as a fast-growing, always-fatal cancer, I prayed that the diagnosis would be wrong and that Clay would recover fully. After the oncologist removed the tumor and had his own lab biopsy it, he said the initial diagnosis was wrong—the cancer was slow-growing and treatable.

God answered my prayer with "Yes." We celebrated with fajitas, called family members with the news, and emailed the 50 families who had been praying for Clay. He has been cancer-free for 12 years.

When I was newly married and working long hours putting my husband through school, I prayed that one day I could work from home and have more time to write as a ministry. Two decades later, that happened.

God answered my prayer with "Wait." I told close friends about the answered prayer. My husband's income increased enough that now I can write nearly full-time.

When my first pregnancy ended in miscarriage, I asked God to not let me miscarry again. But I did.

God answered my prayer with "No." I prayed honestly to God, asking him every question and explaining to him my every fear and hurt. When I miscarried still again, I asked God to help me submit fully to his will. I hung on to the assurance that faithfully enduring hardships gains us an eternal glory that outweighs earthly losses.

YOU HAVE TURNED FOR ME MY *mourning* into *dancing* AND *clothed* me with *gladness*

PSALM 30:11-12

Psalm 30

A Psalm of David. A song at the dedication of the temple.

1 I will extol you, O Lord, for you have drawn me up
    and have not let my foes rejoice over me.
2 O Lord my God, I cried to you for help,
    and you have healed me.
3 O Lord, you have brought up my soul from Sheol;
    you restored me to life from among those who go down to the pit.

4 Sing praises to the Lord, O you his saints,
    and give thanks to his holy name.
5 For his anger is but for a moment,
    and his favor is for a lifetime.
Weeping may tarry for the night,
    but joy comes with the morning.

6 As for me, I said in my prosperity,
    "I shall never be moved."
7 By your favor, O Lord,
    you made my mountain stand strong;
you hid your face;
    I was dismayed.

8 To you, O Lord, I cry,
    and to the Lord I plead for mercy:
9 "What profit is there in my death,
    if I go down to the pit?
Will the dust praise you?
    Will it tell of your faithfulness?
10 Hear, O Lord, and be merciful to me!
    O Lord, be my helper!"

11 You have turned for me my mourning into dancing;
    you have loosed my sackcloth
    and clothed me with gladness,
12 that my glory may sing your praise and not be silent.
    O Lord my God, I will give thanks to you forever!

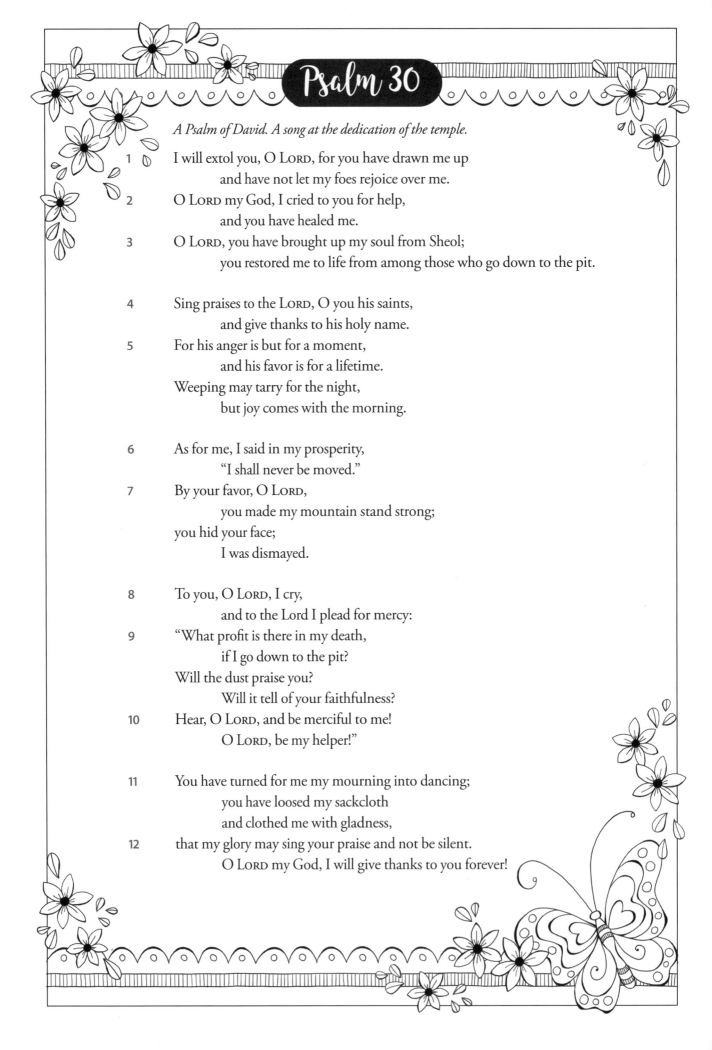

Psalm 146

1   Praise the LORD!
    Praise the LORD, O my soul!
2   I will praise the LORD as long as I live;
            I will sing praises to my God while I have my being.

3   Put not your trust in princes,
            in a son of man, in whom there is no salvation.
4   When his breath departs, he returns to the earth;
            on that very day his plans perish.

5   Blessed is he whose help is the God of Jacob,
            whose hope is in the LORD his God,
6   who made heaven and earth,
            the sea, and all that is in them,
    who keeps faith forever;
7   who executes justice for the oppressed,
            who gives food to the hungry.

    The LORD sets the prisoners free;
8   the LORD opens the eyes of the blind.
    The LORD lifts up those who are bowed down;
            the LORD loves the righteous.
9   The LORD watches over the sojourners;
            he upholds the widow and the fatherless,
            but the way of the wicked he brings to ruin.

10 The LORD will reign forever,
            your God, O Zion, to all generations.
    Praise the LORD!

Years later I wrote what happened next for *Today's Christian Woman*.

> At the fifth miscarriage, I mourned not just the loss of the baby, but the loss of ever bearing children. The lessons I'd learned were helping me to cope, but one question still stymied me. So I prayed: "God, Psalm 37:4 says if I delight myself in you, you'll give me the desires of my heart. I *am* delighting myself in you. I don't understand. Why aren't you giving me the desire of my heart?" Once again I sensed a question to me: "What is the greatest desire of your heart?" My answer came with ease: "Following you, God."
>
> At that moment, I realized all of life involves choosing between conflicting desires. Our choices reveal what we value most. I suddenly understood sacrificial praise (Hebrews 13:15) in a new way: choosing to praise and glorify God by relinquishing something costly. I wanted to offer sacrificial praise, but finding the words was hard, so I pictured my prayer.
>
> I imagined placing my desire for children and the question, "Why?" in a box. I wrapped the box with pale green paper and tied it with gold ribbon, and then placed it at the foot of Jesus' cross, shining softly through a dark night at the bottom of a hill.
>
> I prayed, "This is my gift to you. On Resurrection Day, if you want to open this gift and show me 'Why?'—that's fine. And if you don't, that's fine too—I think answers won't be a priority when I'm overjoyed by being with you."
>
> As the days went on, every time I hurt, every time I yearned, I brought this picture to mind and prayed, "This is my gift to you."[1]

Ironically, to date that story of God saying no has touched more lives and reached more people than any of my stories of God answering yes or wait.

1. Have you had prayers answered yes, wait, or no? Explain.

The psalms we'll read today are **praise psalms**. They'll show us how to honor God when we finally get a job, when the MRI reveals that we're well, when surgery succeeds, when the longed-for baby enters our lives, when a promotion and raise go through, when we can finally buy a first house, when we reconcile with an estranged loved one, when we remember heaven awaits…and when we relinquish our will to the God we know is good.

The first psalm is a **thanksgiving song** David wrote after God answered a prayer with a yes. The second is a **hymn** that describes reasons to praise God. Thanksgiving songs and hymns are the two main types of praise psalms.

Begin your study by praying that God will speak to you through his Word. Think of a time God answered yes. Then read Psalms 30 and 146.[2]

At that moment, I realized all of life involves choosing between conflicting desires. Our choices reveal what we value most.

Initial Thoughts

> **2.** 🎵 What stands out to you from your initial reading of these psalms?

The Big Picture

We'll look at Psalm 30 first.

> **3.** (a) According to the inscription, who wrote Psalm 30? (b) For what occasion does he want it sung?

David bought the land for the future temple after God stopped a plague. The plague was punishment for David displaying pride in and dependence on his vast army (1 Chronicles 21). David and his elders all clothed themselves in sackcloth as they prayed for God to stop the plague. It's possible he wrote this psalm in response to God answering his prayers to stop that plague—that would explain its connection to the temple's dedication.

We don't know for sure, though. As with all psalms, David leaves many of the details vague so they can be sung and prayed by others on many occasions. Perhaps David chose this psalm not because of a direct link, but simply because he wanted the temple dedication to remind everyone of the temple's purpose: drawing near to God, receiving forgiveness of sins, praying to God, and being at peace with God.

Thanksgiving Songs

Thanksgiving songs proclaim public praise for granted prayers.

> **4.** (a) What's a prayer God has answered for you? (b) Has he saved you and forgiven your sins (as in Psalm 51), helped you in discouraging circumstances (Psalms 42–43), or saved you from difficulties (Psalm 71)?

The Little Details
Praise Psalms

Thanksgiving songs are also called **declarative praise psalms** because they publicly declare deliverance. Hymns are also known as **descriptive praise psalms** because they describe God's nature. Some psalms fit into both categories. Here are the psalms Professor Allen P. Ross puts in each category.

Thanksgiving Songs: 18; 21; 30; 32; 34; 40; 41; 66; 106; 116; 138[3]

Hymns: [29]; 36; 105; 111; 113; 117; 135; 136; 146; 147[4]

As with all psalms, David leaves many of the details vague so they can be sung and prayed by others on many occasions.

Thanksgiving songs help us voice praise for answered prayers. Most of these songs contain at least these four elements:

Thanksgiving Song Element	Purpose	Corresponding Verses
1. **Preliminary Praise**	They usually begin with the psalmist's intention to praise God for something	30:1-3
2. **Divine Description**	They describe God's attributes, often with more praise	30:4-5
3. **Dilemma and Deliverance**	They report what was wrong and how God fixed it	30:6-10
4. **Praise Proclamation**	They praise the Lord for the answer to prayer	30:11-12

Each day in this chapter we'll thank God for something using those four elements.

5. 🌙 Think of something for which you're thankful, whether big or small. Write a brief praise using all four of the above elements in whatever order you'd like. Here is an example:

Bless the Lord for calming my father-in-law's fears! He was distraught, but we prayed for the Lord to give him peace, and he did. God is the true peace giver!

The Sacrifice of Praise

In Old Testament times, an Israelite who wanted to show gratitude for granted prayers and other blessings would bring a **thanksgiving peace offering**—also called a **sacrifice of praise**—to the temple.[5] It consisted of a perfect animal and a mix of breads.[6] Ross says,

> The worshipper would deliver the praise while the sacrifice was on the altar so that the people would know why it was being offered...Then the thankful worshipper would tell his story; and the Levites were always to be prepared to "give thanks" in song when the person finished. Then the worshipper, family and friends, priests and singers, and any poor people present would eat the peace offering as a communal meal.[7]

The testimony that accompanied the offering encouraged the faith of everyone in the temple who heard it. Part of the offering was burned on the altar for God while the rest provided a meal for the worshiper, his relatives and friends, the priests, and the poor. The part burned symbolized sharing the meal with the Lord. Giving portions to the priests and needy gave them a reason for further rejoicing!

6. Read Hebrews 13:15-16. (a) What does Hebrews 13:15 tell us to offer God? (b) How does this verse explain the sacrifice? (c) How often are we to do this? (d) Although Christians no longer make animal and bread sacrifices at a temple that would feed the poor, what does Hebrews 13:16 tell us we must do?

Showing our gratitude to God is tightly tied to sharing what we have with others, including not just friends and family, but also church leaders and the needy.

7. ♩ Begin thinking of ways you can make a sacrifice of praise that involves sharing what you have with others, perhaps with the psalm you'll write. (a) How could you give gifts to the needy so they will know those gifts are a thanksgiving offering for answered prayer? (b) How could you give gifts to your church so those who receive them will know those gifts are a thanksgiving offering for answered prayer? Be ready to discuss this with your small group.

Experiencing Psalms 30 and 146 Creatively

Begin thinking of other ways to interact with Psalms 30 and 146. For inspiration, review Chapter 1, Day 1. Here are some ideas specific to this chapter's psalm:

- On social media, share one of the praises you write as you work through this chapter.
- Have a party in celebration of an answered prayer.
- Bake or buy something special to share with your small group. Attach a tag with one of your praises.
- Spend some time singing your favorite praise songs.

The testimony that accompanied the offering encouraged the faith of everyone in the temple who heard it.

Showing our gratitude to God is tightly tied to sharing what we have with others.

Hope Alive

Our youngest son, Caleb, proposed to his beloved at the lighthouse on the cliffs at Point Loma in San Diego. The historic lighthouse was built to usher ships safely into the bay. By proposing at the lighthouse, Caleb was saying, "I want God to be the lighthouse of our life together." God is a beacon of hope to our lives, and his Word lights our way.

> In the beginning was the Word, and the Word was with God, and the Word was God. He was in the beginning with God. All things were made through him, and without him was not any thing made that was made. In him was life, and the life was the light of men. The light shines in the darkness, and the darkness has not overcome it (John 1:1-5).

Life can change in a flash of lightning: a diagnosis from a doctor; a confession from a spouse or child revealing one of your worst fears; or a pink slip from your employer. In those dark times, we can trade in our fear for faith in God's Word.

I vividly remember our stormiest season. The winds hit our little lifeboat during one of our media tours. Bill wasn't feeling well, so we went to the ER, where a doctor informed him he had high blood pressure. This news caught Bill's attention. His dad had a stroke in his 40s that left him paralyzed, and Bill's grandfather died of a stroke. Later, Bill's personal physician asked, "You're a people helper; if someone came in showing symptoms of escalating blood pressure and had two full-time jobs [pastor and author/speaker], what would you advise?"

Bill solemnly answered, "I have some strategic life choices to make."

It became apparent that God was asking Bill to resign from the lead pastor role he had served in for 15 years. This decision was difficult emotionally and financially. In this same season, Caleb was hit in a football game and rushed to the hospital, where he needed a life-saving blood transfusion. Eight days later, when we brought Caleb home, all I wanted to do was wrap him in my arms. But I had a speaking engagement, which our family needed me to keep.

During my time away, I received calls about my other two sons, who had both also experienced injuries. And the day I returned home, I learned my younger brother was hospitalized after having a heart attack. My stress was welling up like a tidal wave.

When friends would ask, "How are you?" I didn't know how to answer. So I went to the Word and read Psalm 30:5: "Weeping may tarry for the night, but joy comes with the morning." JOY! That's what I needed. I immediately went on a joy hunt. I read Nehemiah 8:10, "The joy of the Lord is your strength," and kept following the well-lit path of joy verses. I studied them and I posted them around my home. I listened to joyful songs. A friend gave me a necklace with the word *joy* on it and I wore it every day.

Joy was becoming my lighthouse of hope.

I now answered "How are you?" with "Choosin' joy!" This saying has caught on with the women who hear me share my story of hope. That's the power of the Word. Its joy is not only your lighthouse; God multiplies the light as you share your hope and praise him.

Flood your life with the word God gives to you. Memorize and meditate on verses that contain that word. It will come alive in your life! You will gain emotional strength and spiritual and practical life insights. And in due course, with the light of God's Word, you *will* see and reach the shore!

Pam

Call Others to Praise!

Thanksgiving songs aren't for solitary occasions. The psalmist not only praises God himself, but calls on others to join him.

> **8.** Read the Psalm30:1-5. What stands out to you the most? Why?

Preliminary Praise

"I will bless the LORD!" "I love you, O LORD!" "Shout for joy to God!" "Oh give thanks to the LORD!" "Praise the LORD!" These are the ways many thanksgiving psalms open. While laments often begin with an introductory cry such as "Save me!" thanksgiving psalms begin with an introductory praise.[8]

> **9.** With what commitment does David begin Psalm 30:1?

That's the purpose of this psalm: extolling the Lord by telling people the good things God has done. To *extol* is to highly praise and exalt. David summarizes why next.

> **10.** (a) What two things had the Lord done for David (30:1)? (b) What had David done (30:2)? (c) How had God responded (30:2)?

The healing may have been physical, spiritual, or emotional.[9] Illnesses were serious matters in David's day, long before penicillin. Sin and apostasy call for spiritual healing. God also heals emotional hurts.

> **11.** (a) What else did the Lord do for David (verse 3)? (b) How does "you have brought up my soul" in verse 3 help explain verse 1?

Saying "you have brought up my soul from Sheol" is like saying, "You yanked me back when I had one foot in the grave." "Sheol" in verse 3a is equivalent to "the pit" in 3b (see sidebar). David's life had been in danger.

> **12.** ♪ (a) What is something for which you would like to praise God? (b) Turn to the My Psalm page at the end of this chapter. Write your name next to "A Psalm of." (c) Write a brief commitment to praise the Lord, followed by a summary of how he helped you. Use Psalm 30:1-3 as a guide.

Divine Description

Thanksgiving songs were meant to accompany public thanksgiving offerings. David now calls on those in the temple to praise the Lord with him for who God is.

> **13.** (a) What two things does David want the people at the temple to do (Psalm 30:4)? (b) What does he call the people?

The word translated *saints* here is sometimes translated *godly ones* or *faithful ones*. It's not referring to the spiritually elite, but to all who faithfully follow God and aim to obey his commands. In the New Testament, everyone redeemed by Jesus is called a saint (Colossians 1:12-13), so consider Psalm 30:4 as David calling *you* to praise God!

"To his holy name" in the Hebrew is literally "to the memorial of his holiness."[11] Public thanksgiving memorializes God's acts and so makes known his name.

David wants us to sing praises and give thanks. These are two of the many ways the psalms call us to respond to God's goodness. Other psalms tell us to shout for joy or praise aloud his mighty deeds; to play stringed instruments or sound cymbals loudly; to clap our hands or dance with joy; to bow down heads or lift up hands. In other words, get active!

David next describes what he has learned about God. These attributes are a reason for praising him.

> **14.** Why should we praise God, according to Psalm 30:5?

David has faced God's disciplining anger and has learned that God's anger is brief compared to his favor. He has wept many nights, but joy has greeted him later.

Let's look at what the New Testament says about God's discipline.

The Little Details
Sheol

According to Allen P. Ross, the word translated *Sheol* has different meanings:

- the grave
- death
- extreme danger (as in Psalm 30)
- hell or hades, the realm of the departed who "are cut off from fellowship with God"[10]

Everyone redeemed by Jesus is called a saint, so consider Psalm 30:4 as David calling *you* to praise God!

---

15. Read Hebrews 12:8-11 below and then underline the answers to these questions. (a) Does any true child of God escape God's discipline (verse 8)? (b) Why does God discipline us (verse 10)? (c) How does God's discipline seem when we're in the midst of it (verse 11)? (d) What does it yield later (verse 11)?

> [8]If you are left without discipline, in which all have participated, then you are illegitimate children and not sons. [9]Besides this, we have had earthly fathers who disciplined us and we respected them. Shall we not much more be subject to the Father of spirits and live? [10]For they disciplined us for a short time as it seemed best to them, but he disciplines us for our good, that we may share his holiness. [11]For the moment all discipline seems painful rather than pleasant, but later it yields the peaceful fruit of righteousness to those who have been trained by it.

Let's finish up by writing a short song or prayer of thanksgiving before continuing our psalm.

16. ♩ Think of a way God has healed you emotionally, physically, or spiritually. Write a brief praise using the four thanksgiving song elements: preliminary praise, divine description, dilemma and deliverance, and praise proclamation.

17. ♫ (a) What did you learn about God through the circumstance about which you're writing your psalm? (b) When you think about how he blessed you, what two praise responses do you most feel like giving (shouting for joy, praising aloud, singing, dancing, playing instruments, bowing down, lifting hands, and so on)? (c) Turn to the My Psalm page. Leave a blank space and write a line calling others to praise God through the two praise responses you just named. (d) Write another line or two describing what you learned is the reason others should join you in praise.

Tell of God's Deeds!

David has announced his intention to praise God, summarized what went wrong and how God helped, and described God's attributes. Now he's going to give us the details of his deliverance.

> **18.** Read Psalm 30's last three stanzas (verses 6-12). What stands out to you the most? Why?

Dilemma and Deliverance

David now tells us more details about his former troubles, including what was wrong and how he prayed.

What Was Wrong

> **19.** When things were going well for David, what did he say (Psalm 30:6)?

Uh-oh.

At the least, thinking we can never be moved is naive. But since David speaks of God's anger, he is likely confessing sin here, either the sin of self-sufficiency ("I've got so much going for me I don't need to rely on God") or of pride ("I'm God's man of power of the hour").

> **20.** Read the following verses and underline in them what we should avoid.
>
> **Pride in material blessings:**
>
> "Beware lest you say in your heart, 'My power and the might of my hand have gotten me this wealth.' You shall remember the LORD your God, for it is he who gives you power to get wealth" (Deuteronomy 8:17-18).
>
> **Pride in spiritual giftedness:**
>
> "Who sees anything different in you? What do you have that you did not receive? If then you received it, why do you boast as if you did not receive it?" (1 Corinthians 4:7).
>
> **Pride in being above falling:**
>
> "Let anyone who thinks that he stands take heed lest he fall" (1 Corinthians 10:12).

In the next verse, consider "mountain" to be the Mount Zion fortress from which David ruled; it's figurative for all his success.

> **21.** (a) According to Psalm 30:7, why had David been so strong? (b) What happened when God hid his face? (c) How did that show David the true source of his strength?

Sometimes God hides his face and stops bestowing favor for a time. Here, he did it to purify David's character. Of course, God doesn't literally hide his face: The expression is an **anthropomorphism,** an assigning of a human trait to God to communicate a truth about him, in this case about his favor. The result was that David realized his total dependence on God.

The Prayer God Answered

David now tells us the prayer God answered.

> **22.** (a) When David realized his error, what was his response (verse 8)? (b) Mercy is not getting the punishment we deserve. How does David's plea show newfound humility?

This verse can be translated either in the past tense ("I cried") so that it introduces the prayer of verses 9-11, or in the present tense, so that it is the first line of the prayer.[12] Either way, David records here the prayer he says God answered.

In verse 9, David presents reasons God would want to answer his prayer: "What profit is there in my death, if I go down to the pit? Will the dust praise you? Will it tell of your faithfulness?" This isn't crass bargaining. When our prayers include reasons God might want to answer our requests, the reasons strengthen our hope and assure us we're praying according to God's revealed will. Here David is saying if he lives he can praise God and tell others of God's faithfulness, which would glorify God. If he dies, this can't happen.

> **23.** (a) What two things does David want the Lord to be (verse 10)? (b) How does this acknowledge his lack of self-sufficiency?

When our prayers include reasons God might want to answer our requests, the reasons strengthen our hope and assure us we're praying according to God's revealed will.

24. ♫ (a) What caused the trouble that is the subject of the psalm you're writing? (b) Turn to the My Psalm page, leave a blank space, and write a couple of lines explaining your dilemma. (c) Leave another blank space and record how you prayed for help.

Praise Proclamation

Now David joyfully praises his God.

25. What three things has God done for David (Psalm 30:11)?

In ancient days, Israelites wore a coarse fabric called sackcloth as a sign of mourning. It was woven from dark goat's hair.[13] Imagine wearing burlap instead of black for mourning.

26. (a) Why had God answered his prayer, according to David (verse 12)? (b) What does this tell us about the importance of telling others about our answered prayers?

"My glory" is David's way of referring to his innermost self—his spirit.[14] That which God had made glorious in David glorifies God.

God hadn't answered David's prayer for David's sake alone. No, he answered it so all those who heard David sing of God's mercies and help would place their hope in God. Those who didn't know God might turn to him, and those who did might have their faith strengthened. That is why we need to tell others when God answers our prayers!

27. In 2 Corinthians 1:4 below, underline the reason God comforts us when we're afflicted.

[God] comforts us in all our affliction, so that we may be able to comfort those who are in any affliction, with the comfort with which we ourselves are comforted by God.

28. What does David commit to doing in Psalm 30:12b?

God answered David's prayer so all those who heard David sing of God's mercies and help would place their hope in God.

The Little Details
Hanukkah

Jews now use Psalm 30 to celebrate Hanukkah, the holiday also known as the Festival of Lights and the Feast of the Dedication (John 10:22). This annual festival was not part of the Mosaic Law. It commemorates the rededication of the temple in 164 BC after Judas Maccabeus led a successful revolt against Antiochus Epiphanes, who had defiled the temple by sacrificing pigs to Zeus in it.

David does not take his deliverance lightly; he commits to calling to mind his deliverance throughout his life so he can again give thanks.

> **29.** ♩ (a) Name an answered prayer for which you will be eternally thankful. (b) Write a brief praise for it using the four thanksgiving song elements: preliminary praise, divine description, dilemma and deliverance, and praise proclamation.

Have you noticed that enjoyment is not complete until you've expressed and shared it?

I didn't always know this. I confess that the first few times I read Psalms, I wondered why God commanded people to praise him. The idea made me squirm because I associated it with tyrannical dictators and bad bosses: people who surround themselves with yes-men, reward flattery, and punish disagreement. Since then I've found I wasn't alone in my confusion.

What I missed was that the psalms aren't filled with God demanding that people praise him. Rather, the psalmists are godly people who experienced the wonders and realities of God, and who responded naturally with praise and with calling others to witness and share their delight.

C.S. Lewis put it this way:

> All enjoyment spontaneously overflows into praise unless (sometimes even if) shyness or the fear of boring others is deliberately brought in to check it. The world rings with praise—lovers praising their mistresses, readers their favourite poet, walkers praising the countryside, players praising their favourite game—praise of weather, wines, dishes, actors, motors, horses, colleges, countries, historical personages, children, flowers, mountains, rare stamps, rare beetles, even sometimes politicians or scholars...Just as men spontaneously praise whatever they value, so they spontaneously urge us to join them in praising it: "Isn't she lovely? Wasn't it glorious? Don't you think that magnificent?" The Psalmists in telling everyone to praise God are doing what all men do when they speak of what they care about.[15]

It's time for us to likewise commemorate deliverance.

> **30.** ♫ Consider the deliverance you are writing your psalm about and reflect on how you prayed before deliverance came. (a) Turn to the My Psalm page. Skip a line and describe how God changed your situation (see Psalm 30:11). (b) Finally, write a line expressing why God helped you and a commitment to be thankful forever (use Psalm 30:12 as a model).

Enjoyment is not complete until you've expressed and shared it.

Praise the Lord!

Whereas thanksgiving songs praise God for answering a specific prayer, **hymns** praise God for who he is and what he's done in human history.

When times are good, singing and praying hymns seems natural to those fully aware of God's hand in their lives and in history. How can our hearts not burst forth with praise to the Giver of our good?

If times are good but we've begun to think what we have is by our own hand, then hymns remind us who gave us all the good gifts we have and correct our attitude so we don't need the discipline David described in Psalm 30.

When times are troubled, hymns focus our attention on the greatness and goodness of God so we remember why we hope. They remind us of God's character and his saving acts. They show us the bigger picture: a creation of animals and angels, hills and heavens, stones and stars, grasshoppers and galaxies. Our own stories find their place in the story of creation, redemption, and coming exaltation. Hymns provide perspective: We are not the center of history—God the Creator is.

> **31.** Read Psalm 146. What stands out to you the most? Why?

Hymns often have three sections:

Hymn Element	Purpose	Corresponding Verses
1. Call to Praise	Hymns begin with an opening invitation to praise	146:1-2
2. Cause for Praise	The main body of hymns describes God and his acts as the reason to praise him	146:5-9
3. Conclusion	Hymns often end with an affirmation of faith or renewed call to praise	146:10

Psalm 146 is the first of the group of five hymns that are the **grand doxology** for the entire Psalter. Just as Psalms 1 and 2 introduce the Psalter, so these five psalms conclude it.[16]

Let's look more deeply into Psalm 146.

When times are troubled, hymns focus our attention on the greatness and goodness of God so we remember why we hope.

The Little Details
Doxologies

All five books of Psalms close with a praise that is not part of the psalm that precedes it, but is the **doxology** (a short praise) concluding that book:

- Book I: Psalm 41:13
- Book II: Psalm 72:18-19
- Book III: Psalm 89:52
- Book IV: Psalm 106:48
- Book V: Psalm 150:6[17]

Call to Praise

Psalm 146 can be outlined like this:

A   Call to praise (verses 1-2)

    B   Men as princes who perish (verses 3-4)

        C   God the Creator (verses 5-6b)

            D   God keeps faith forever (verse 6c)

        C′   God the Sustainer (verses 7-9)

    B′   God as King forever (verse 10a-b)

A′   Call to praise (verse 10c)

> **32.** What does Psalm 146:1a call us to do?

Your Bible may say "Praise the LORD!" or "Hallelujah!" The English word *hallelujah* is a transliteration of the two Hebrew words that mean "praise the Lord." All the psalms in the Psalter's doxology (Psalms 146–150) begin and end with this glorious call to praise. Because of this, they are sometimes called the Hallelujah Psalms.

> **33.** (a) In Psalm 146:1, "my soul" is the psalmist's way of addressing himself. Who is the psalmist telling to praise the Lord? (b) What does the psalmist commit to do (1:2)?

> **34.** ◖ Can you commit to lifelong praise to God? Explain.

Men as Princes Who Perish

Do you ever wonder if getting just the right people into government would solve your nation's problems? Are you ever frustrated with government officials? Have you struggled under the authority of an unjust CEO? The psalmist speaks to that next.

> **35.** (a) What does the psalmist warn us not to do (Psalm 146:3a)? (b) In verse 3b, what does he call a prince (or ruler)? (c) Why (verse 4)?

This was a big issue at the time the Psalter was compiled in its final form with this psalm as part of the doxology. The Israelites had neither their own nation nor their own king (see sidebar). They served under a foreign power. They longed for the Messiah to appear, set them free from bondage to other nations, and rule them justly.

> **36.** 🌙 (a) In what ways do leaders disappoint today? (b) How does this affect your longing for the day we'll be under Jesus' rule in the new heaven and earth? (c) How does Jesus differ from the princes described in verses 3-4?

God the Creator

The psalmist now begins to tell us why we should praise God.

> **37.** Who is blessed, according to Psalm 146:5?

Jacob was one of the patriarchs. He was later renamed "Israel," and all Jews descend from him. The Jews would be familiar with the stories of how God helped Jacob when his brother sought to kill him and his uncle repeatedly cheated him. God blessed and sustained him. God also molded Jacob's character. Calling God "the God of Jacob" reminds us that if God could bless Jacob in difficult circumstances, he can bless us.

> **38.** What has God done that shows him to be more powerful than any human prince (verse 6a-b)?

God Keeps Faith Forever

> **39.** (a) What does God do that no human ruler can do (verse 6c)? (b) What are two ways he does this (verse 7)?

Even King David failed to perfectly execute justice, as we saw in our look at Psalm 51, where David repented of his sins of adultery and murder. And although for the most part

The Little Details

Themes of the Psalter's Books

Book I of the Psalter (Psalms 3–41, excluding the introduction) traces the rise of David's kingdom. All but two psalms are ascribed to David, and the two that aren't (9 and 33) are related to the psalms immediately before them and so may be by David as well. Many of the laments concern his travails before becoming king.

Book II (Psalms 42–72) is the establishment of the kingdom under David and his son Solomon. It ends with a royal psalm by Solomon.

Book III (Psalms 73–89) mourns the fall of the kingdom. It was probably compiled during the exile that followed the destruction of Jerusalem and the temple in 586 BC. It contains the most heartbreaking of the psalms and ends asking God why he has rejected his people.

Books IV (Psalms 90–106) and **V** (Psalms 107–145, excluding the doxology) were compiled after the people returned to the land in 538 BC. They answer the questions of Book III and acknowledge God as King.

he ruled righteously, he eventually died and passed the throne on to others, some who were good rulers and some who weren't.

One of the ways God executes justice and gives food to the hungry is through us. According to 2 Corinthians 5:20, we are his representatives on earth: "We are ambassadors for Christ, God making his appeal through us."

God commands us to stand up for the oppressed and feed the poor. When we pray psalms that talk about how good God is for righting wrongs and feeding the hungry, we should consider that proclaiming these acts as good should commit us to doing them. Acting as God's representative by caring for those he cares for is an act of worship.

We'll finish Psalm 146 on Day 5. Let's end today with thanksgiving.

> **40.** ♪ What is something for which you are thankful today? Write a brief praise using the four thanksgiving song elements: preliminary praise, divine description, dilemma and deliverance, and praise proclamation.

God commands us to stand up for the oppressed and feed the poor.

Worshiping with Praise Psalms

On Day 4, we saw in Psalm 146 the beginning call to praise, the exhortation not to trust in princes who perish, and descriptions of God as Creator and the One who keeps faith forever. But the psalmist isn't done with his reasons to praise God.

God the Sustainer

In the next stanza, the psalmist continues his list of reasons we should praise God.

> **41.** Read the psalmist's list of actions God takes for which we should praise him (Psalm 146:6-9). Which is most comforting to you today? Why?

In this study, we've seen many examples of how God acts for us. Compare what we've seen to the verses you just read and ponder how God has acted in your life.

- *God keeps faith forever:* Psalm 1 tells us God knows and watches our ways. Psalm 2 reminds us of the coming eternal kingdom where Jesus will reign forever. Psalm 51 assures us God will not break faith with those who have a broken and contrite heart. Psalm 23 describes God's faithful care. Psalm 73 displays how God keeps our feet from slipping. Psalms 42–43 show how to pray with hope that we will again praise God on the other side of our dilemma. Psalm 71 shows God's tender care from our youth to old age. Psalm 30 reminds us of answered prayers. *How have you seen God's faithfulness?*

- *God executes justice:* Psalm 71 shows God answering the prayer of one unjustly attacked. Psalms 30 and 51 show God disciplining followers who erred. Psalms 2 and 73 speak of God's final execution of justice on judgment day. *Have you experienced discipline and vindication?*

- *God gives food to the hungry:* Psalm 23 describes the Lord providing sustenance as a Shepherd to his sheep, showing that God gives us physical and spiritual food. Psalm 30 shows a worshiper giving public thanks, which by God's command included giving food to the poor. *Has God provided for your physical and spiritual needs?*

- *God sets prisoners free:* The psalmist who wrote Psalms 42–43 had been unjustly captured and taken from his home. That his psalm was deposited at the temple tells us God likely answered his prayer for release with a yes. *Has God freed you from an oppressive situation?*

- *God opens the eyes of the blind:* In Psalm 73 Asaph was spiritually blind until he went to the house of God. *How has God opened your spiritual eyes?*

- *God lifts up those who are bowed down:* David bowed down in repentance in

Psalm 51, and God forgave and raised him. In Psalms 42–43, the psalmist's soul is cast (or bowed) down, but he hopes in the God who is his salvation. Psalm 71 praises God for lifting the psalmist from earth's depths and restoring his honor. *How has God exalted you from a lowly position?*

- *God loves the righteous:* Psalm 1 describes God's love for those who walk in his ways. *Do you sense God's love for you?*

- *God watches over sojourners:* In Psalms 42–43, God gave a comforting prayer song to one trapped in a country not his own. *Has God comforted you when you were far from home?*

- *God upholds the widow and the fatherless:* Psalm 23 describes the Lord's tender care as a Shepherd leading and protecting his sheep. *Have you known bereavement or abandonment, yet tasted of God's tender care?*

- *God ruins the way of the wicked.* Psalms 1 and 2 describe this. *Have you seen the plans of the wicked fail?*

> **42.** ◗ Which of these instances of God's care in the psalms we've looked at brings you the most comfort? Why?

If we praise God for these actions, we affirm that the actions are good. They are, therefore, actions we should imitate. After all, we are God's representatives on earth.

> **43.** ◗ Which of the instances of God's care in the psalms could you extend to someone this week?

The psalmist adds one more reason to praise God.

God as King Forever

Even the godly kings couldn't live forever, and they couldn't guarantee their sons would rule righteously. In fact, at the time this psalm was placed in the doxology, the actions of a series of wicked kings had brought God's judgment and the end of the monarchy. The earthly kings had failed miserably in their job of ruling with justice and glorifying God to the nations so that others would come to him.

The earthly kings had failed miserably in their job of ruling with justice and glorifying God to the nations.

44. (a) For how long will the Lord reign, according to Psalm 146:10a-b? (b) And what does the psalmist conclude is the only proper response to this (146:10c)?

The psalmist ends with the same call with which he began, forming an **enclosure** that frames the reasons to praise the Lord.

While the Israelites waited for God to send the Messiah, no matter how disappointed they were in the injustices and persecutions of the empires under which they served, they could remember that God reigns from heaven forever.

Likewise, when we're disappointed in earthly leaders, this psalm gives us hope.

But there's more. When Messiah Jesus finally came, he said his kingdom was not of this world. He spoke of the kingdom of heaven and promised eternal life to all those who trust in him. In that kingdom we will eat from the Tree of Life, put on incorruptible bodies, revel in perfect justice, reunite with lost loved ones, and dwell in the presence of the holy God.

Concluding Words

We've worshiped with multiple psalm genres in this series—wisdom, royal, messianic, penitential, confidence, and lament—and we'll finish with thanksgiving songs and hymns. They are psalms for all seasons of life, psalms that build hope.

45. ♩ What have you learned from the psalms we've looked at in this series for which you are thankful? Write a brief praise using the four thanksgiving song elements: preliminary praise, divine description, dilemma and deliverance, and praise proclamation.

Worshiping with Sacrifices of Praise

What better way to end our study than with glorifying our great God?

We glorify God when we declare to others his answers to our prayers. We glorify God when we describe to others his goodness and his saving acts. We glorify God when we care for the poor, sick, and oppressed, letting it be known we do so as God's representative because he cares for the poor, sick, and oppressed.

46. ♩ How will you publicly glorify God with your thanksgiving song and a thank offering?

In God's kingdom we will eat from the Tree of Life, put on incorruptible bodies, revel in perfect justice, reunite with lost loved ones, and dwell in the presence of the holy God.

Worshiping with Praise Psalms

Today we will worship God with praise psalms that glorify him before heavenly creatures.

Psalm 30

We begin with a song of thanksgiving that declares God's answer to prayer.

- Find a quiet place and prepare your heart, mind, and body for worship. Go outside or near a window so you see God's creation.
- *Optional*: Begin by worshiping God in song.
- If anything is weighing on you, take it to your heavenly Father, who loves you.
- Turn to Psalm 30 and pray through it aloud.
- **Praise** God for his favor that lasts a lifetime; **confess** anything that convicts you; **ask** God for help in extolling him; and **thank** God for clothing you with gladness.

Psalm 146

Psalm 146 is a hymn that describes how great God is.

- Turn to Psalm 146 and pray it aloud, letting the meaning of the words carry you into worship.

Psalms 147–150

In Psalm 146, we called ourselves to praise the Lord. In the remainder of the doxology, we'll call others.

- Ponder the lament psalms and what you have prayed for over these weeks. Then pray Psalm 147, a hymn that calls all God's people to praise him for his great care.
- Recall the wisdom and confidence psalms and the hope they build. Now turn to Psalm 148 and pray it, calling all creation to praise God with you.
- Think back to the royal and messianic Psalm 2, which links to the second-to-last psalm in another enclosure. Pray Psalm 149, and join in calling all God's people to praise him and look toward the coming of his kingdom.
- Remember entering the Psalter with a Torah psalm instructing us how to be blessed. Finish the Psalter with Psalm 150's natural and right response to having been blessed.

My Psalm

- Offer your thanksgiving psalm to God in worship.

The Lord: He is good! Hallelujah!

We glorify God when we declare to others his answers to our prayers.

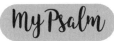

My Psalm

A Psalm of:

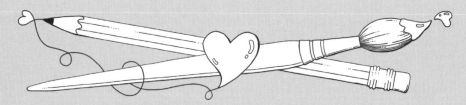

Creative Connection

When we count our blessings and praise God for answered prayers, joy tends to naturally well up in our hearts, doesn't it? Reading through this chapter's lessons on Psalm 30 and thinking about some of the prayers God has answered for me over the years made me want to do a happy dance, and thus this chapter's illustration!

I love looking for ways to use symbolism in my art, using imagery to express meaning and emotion. Psalm 30:11 provided the perfect opportunity. The emotions I wanted to express here were joy and freedom—the joy that comes when we see God's hand at work in our lives and the freedom we enjoy through praise and thanksgiving. For me, this girl exudes joy! Her heart's desire is to proclaim what God has done as she dances joyfully across the page, raising up her testimony for all to see. The scattering of the flowers adds to her sense of delight, and the butterfly gracefully symbolizes the freedom we experience as we trust in God's promises and provision.

The truth is that this illustration wasn't easy for me. To make it appear as though my girl is in motion and the banners are flowing in the wind required a good bit of drawing and erasing...and erasing and drawing...until I got it just right. I oftentimes will draw several rough sketches of the same verse or design before I decide on the one I want to finish and show the world. So don't be afraid to sketch just for fun. Sketching is your friend—and so is your eraser. Making preliminary drawings in a sketchbook allows you the freedom to play and make mistakes, which are just part of the process. And the more you practice drawing, the more confident you will become and the more fun you will have.

👁 Discover more creative inspiration.

Karla

You have turned for me my mourning into dancing and clothed me with gladness

O LORD my God I will give thanks to you forever

PSALM 30:11-12

Tips for Committing Scripture to Heart

The more senses we involve when we're learning something, the better and faster we learn it. Here is a list of creative tips for committing Scripture to heart. Try as few or as many as you want.

Pictures

Draw pictures from the verses that will later trigger your memory. Add something in each picture that represents something in the next picture so they link together, forming a sequence you can remember.

Prompts

On a separate piece of paper, write the initial letters of the words in the psalm you are memorizing. Say the verses using only the letters as prompts. If you forget a part, look back at your sketches. Repeat until you can say the psalm twice in a row correctly.

⦿ Download the initial letter prompts for Psalm 23.

Recording

Record yourself saying the psalm on your mobile phone. Speak slowly, distinctly, and with meaning. Play it back while trying to say the words along with the playback. Use the pictures as prompts.

Writing

Read the psalm aloud as you write it or type it, looking at the text as little as possible. Then try to write it looking only at the pictures. Finally, write it without prompts by bringing the pictures into your mind's eye.

Notes

Chapter 1—Psalm 1: The Hope of God's Blessing

1. Line breaks and indents are from Allen P. Ross, *A Commentary on the Psalms,* 3 vols. (Grand Rapids: Kregel, 2011–2016), 1:181–182. Stanza breaks are from the NIV.

2. Willem A. VanGemeren, *The Expositor's Bible Commentary,* vol. 5, *Psalms,* ed. Tremper Longman III and David E. Garland, rev. ed. (Grand Rapids: Zondervan, 2008), 77.

3. Allen P. Ross, *A Commentary on the Psalms,* 3 vols. (Grand Rapids: Kregel, 2011–2016), 1:185.

4. Ibid., 1:193–194.

5. Ibid., 185–186.

6. Psalm 94:12; Philippians 2:13; Hebrews 12:11; 1 John 3:10.

7. Mark D. Futato, *Handbooks for Old Testament Exegesis, Interpreting the Psalms: An Exegetical Handbook,* ed. David M. Howard Jr. (Grand Rapids: Kregel, 2007), 58.

8. "The word 'law'...can refer to instruction in general, or an individual teaching, or the commandments, or the books of the Law, or Scriptures as a whole." Ross, *Psalms,* 1:188.

9. Timothy Trammel, *Holman Illustrated Bible Dictionary,* ed. Chad Brand, Charles Draper, Archie England (Nashville: Holman, 2003), s.v. "Palestine."

10. See the parable of the sower in Luke 8:6,13.

11. D.A. Carson, *The Pillar New Testament Commentary: The Gospel According to John* (Grand Rapids: Eerdmans, 1991), 256.

12. Ross, *Psalms,* 1:193.

13. Gordon J. Wenham, *Psalms as Torah: Reading Biblical Song Ethically* (Grand Rapids: Baker Academic, 2012), 82.

14. Douglas J. Moo, *The New International Commentary on the New Testament: The Epistle to the Romans,* ed. Ned B. Stonehouse, F.F. Bruce, and Gordon D. Fee (Grand Rapids: Eerdmans, 1996), 751.

15. Ibid., 752–753.

16. Wenham, *Psalms as Torah,* 57.

Chapter 2—Psalm 2: The Hope of Messiah's Reign

1. Line breaks, segment breaks, and indents are from Ross, *Psalms,* 1:197-198, with the exception of separating 7a into its own stanza. That and the stanza breaks are from NIV.

2. John 14:30; Ephesians 2:2; Revelation 12:9-10.

3. Robert Alter, *The Art of Biblical Poetry,* rev. ed. (New York: Basic Books, 2011), 8.

4. Futato, *Interpreting the Psalms,* 31-32.

5. *The NIV Study Bible,* 2011 ed. (Grand Rapids: Zondervan, 2011), s.v. "1 Kings 1:39."

6. John 5:19; John 16:11; Revelation 2:13. Adam and Eve were supposed to reign over the earth.

7. Ross, *Psalms,* 1:205.

8. Hebrews 12:22.

9. Ross, *Psalms,* 1:210.

10. R. Laird Harris, Gleason L. Archer, Bruce K. Waltke, ed., "2401: שָׁלֵם," in *Theological Wordbook of the Old Testament* (Chicago: Moody Press, 1980), WORD*search* CROSS e-book, 932.

11. Isaiah 9:6-7; Revelation 11:15; Ephesians 2:19-22; 1 Peter 2:5; Hebrews 3:3-6; Ephesians 2:14-18.

12. Revelation 20:14-15; 21:8.

13. Jack W. Hayford, *Worship His Majesty* (Waco: Word Books, 1987), 168.

14. Allen P. Ross, *Recalling the Hope of Glory: Biblical Worship from the Garden to the New Creation* (Grand Rapids: Kregel, 2006), 50–51.

15. Ibid., 52.

Chapter 3—Psalm 51: The Hope of Mercy

1. Gordon Wenham, *The Psalter Reclaimed: Praying and Praising with the Psalms* (Wheaton: Crossway, 2013), 50.

2. Chapter titles are from the *Holman Christian Standard Bible* (Nashville: Holman Bible Publishers, 2008), WORD*search* CROSS e-book.

3. Stanza breaks are from the NIV.

4. David became king in Hebron at age 30 and moved to Jerusalem around 37–38 (2 Samuel 5:4-5). *The NIV Study Bible* places these events about ten years after the move to Jerusalem (s.v. "2 Samuel 11:1").

5. Robert D. Bergen, *New American Commentary—Volume 7: 1, 2 Samuel* (Nashville: Broadman and Holman, 2002), WORD*search* CROSS e-book, s.v. "2 Samuel 11:1."

6. Ross, *Psalms*, 2:180-182.

7. Exodus 34:6-7. For a full treatment of this passage, see http://jeanejones.net/2012/05/sins-of-the-fathers/.

8. Ross, *Psalms*, 2:176-177.

9. Billy Graham, "Answers," *Billy Graham Evangelistic Association*, last modified May 15, 2009, http://billygraham.org/answer/how-often-should-we-ask-god-to-forgive-us-should-we-ask-him-every-day-i-know-were-supposed-to-trust-jesus-for-our-forgiveness-and-i-have-but-im-not-perfect/.

10. Clay Jones, "Original Sin: Its Importance and Fairness," *Christian Research Journal* 34:6 (2011). A copy of the article can be found here: http://www.equip.org/article/original-sin-its-importance-and-fairness/#christian-books-3.

11. Ross, *Psalms*, 2:190.

12. E.W.G. Masterman, *The International Standard Bible Encyclopedia*, ed. James Orr (Chicago: Howard-Severance Co., 1915), s.v. "HYSSOP," WORD*search* CROSS e-book.

13. John 16:7; 2 Timothy 1:14; 1 Corinthians 6:19.

14. For more on receiving God's forgiveness, see Clay Jones on So You've Sinned Again…and Again: http://www.clayjones.net/2011/06/so-you%E2%80%99ve-sinned-again%E2%80%A6-and-again/.

15. Ross, *Hope of Glory*, 199.

16. The words applied to both the "unclean" food before Peter and the "unclean" people to whom God was sending Peter to preach the gospel.

17. David's oldest, Amnon, could have been 17.

18. Bergen, *NAC*, s.v. "2 Samuel 12:7-10."

19. Ibid., s.v. "1 Samuel 25:39b-44."

20. Ross, *Hope of Glory*, 198-204.

Chapter 4—Psalm 23: The Hope of the Lord's Good Care

1. Wenham, *Psalms as Torah*, 46.

2. Futato, *Interpreting the Psalms*, 161.

3. Stanza breaks, line breaks, segment breaks, and indents are from Ross, *Psalms*, 1:181-182.

4. Ibid., 559.

5. Phillip Keller, *A Shepherd Looks at Psalm 23* (Grand Rapids: Daybreak, 1970), 35.

6. Deuteronomy 8:3.

7. Isaiah 1:18; Isaiah 53:6; Ezekiel 34:16,21-22; Jeremiah 31:25.

8. Keller, *Psalm 23*, 57.

9. Ibid., 71–72.

10. Chad Brand, Charles Draper, Archie England, ed., *Holman Illustrated Bible Dictionary* (Nashville: Holman Bible Publishers, 2003), WORD*search* CROSS e-book, s.v. "Valley."

11. Keller, *Psalm 23*, 93, 98.

12. Ibid., 93.

13. See Leviticus 27:32 and Keller, *Psalm 23*, 95–96.

14. Keller, *Psalm 23*, 96.

15. Ibid., 101.

16. Ibid., 103.

17. Ibid., 100.

18. Ibid.

19. Ross, *Psalms*, 1:567.

20. Ibid., 568.

21. For David, "the house of the Lord" probably referred to the Tent of Meeting. After Solomon built the temple, the phrase referred to the temple.

22. Ross, *Psalms*, 1:278.

Chapter 5—Psalm 73: Hope When Life Seems Unfair

1. Job 12:5 NIV.

2. 1 Chronicles 16:4-7; 25:2,7.

3. See 1 Chronicles 16:5 and Ross, *Hope of Glory*, 257.

4. Stanza breaks, line breaks, segment breaks, and indents are from the NIV.

5. VanGemeren, *Expositor's*, 562. NIV: "From their callous hearts comes iniquity."

6. James 3:14-16.

7. 2 Corinthians 4:17; 1 Peter 1:4.

Chapter 6—Psalms 42–43: Finding Hope When Downcast

1. Ross, *Psalms,* 2:15.

2. Line breaks, segment breaks, and indents are from Ross, *Psalms*, 2:11-15, except for verse 6, which follows ESV (ESV and NIV have "and my God" ending the previous line, while Ross (*Psalms*), KJV, and NASB have "O my God" beginning the next line). Stanza breaks are from the NIV.

3. Other possibilities are "an efficacious song," "a meditation," or "a skillful psalm." Ross, *Psalms*, 1:48.

4. Andrew J. Schmutzer and David M. Howard Jr, gen. ed., *The Psalms: Language for All Seasons of the Soul* (Chicago: Moody Publishers, 2013), 128–129. Adapted.

5. Ross, *Psalms*, 1:111-114.

6. In the Hebrew manuscripts, there's a slight difference between 42:5 and the other two instances of the refrain, but most translations don't show the difference.

7. Ross, *Psalms*, 2:23.

8. Ibid., 2:26.

9. Ibid., 2:14n19.

10. Ross, *Psalms*, 1:113.

11. Ibid., 2:31.

12. D. Martyn Lloyd-Jones, *Spiritual Depression: Its Causes and Its Cure* (Grand Rapids: Eerdmans, 1987), 220–221.

13. Ross, *Hope of Glory*, 184.

Chapter 7—Psalm 71: Continual Hope

1. Stanza breaks are from the NIV.

2. Ross, *Psalms,* 1:687-688.

3. Romans 8:24-25

4. "Those who hope in me will not be disappointed" (Isaiah 49:23 NIV). Also Romans 5:5.

5. Consider 1 Corinthians 15:19; Hebrews 11:24-26,32-33,39-40; and John 12:25.

6. 1 Corinthians 4:5; 1 Corinthians 15:42-44; Matthew 13:41; Revelation 21:4; John 14:2; 1 Peter 1:4; Matthew 5:12; 1 Corinthians 3:12-14; Revelation 21:3.

Chapter 8—Psalms 30 and 146: Hope Fulfilled

1. Jean E. Jones, "Journey of Childlessness," *Today's Christian Woman,* April 2010 (http://www.todayschristianwoman.com/articles/2010/april/journeychildlessness.html).

2. Text, breaks, and indents are from the ESV.

3. Ross, *Psalms,* 1:123.

4. Ross, *Psalms,* 1:124. Ross's list names Psalm 28 rather than 29, but this is a typographical error as can be seen from the commentary, which calls 28 a lament and 29 descriptive praise.

5. Ibid., 2:166.

6. Leviticus 7:11-34. The thank offering was a type of peace (or fellowship) offering. Peace offerings celebrated being at peace with God.

7. Ross, *Hope of Glory,* 272.

8. Ross, *Psalms,* 1:123.

9. Ibid., 1:669n19.

10. Ibid., 1:267n22.

11. English Standard Version text note, s.v. "Psalm 30:4."

12. Ross, *Psalms,* 1:676. Most translations use the past tense so that the phrase introduces the prayer.

13. Merrill Unger, *The New Unger's Bible Dictionary* (Chicago: Moody Press, 1957), s.v. "SACKCLOTH," WORD*search* CROSS e-book.

14. Ross, *Psalms,* 1:678.

15. C.S. Lewis, *The Inspirational Writings of C.S. Lewis, Reflections on the Psalms* (New York: Inspirational Press, 1994), 179.

16. Ross, *Psalms,* 1:50-51, 61.

17. Ibid., 1:50.

Acknowledgments

Pam Farrel

To God, thank you for reaching, rebuilding, and reviving my life through the power of your Word! To Jean and Karla, thank you for being faithful stewards of your amazing talents. I am a better leader with you both in my life! To Hope, LaRae, Barb, Kathleen, Bob Hawkins, and the Harvest House team for believing in a unique product that connects Bible study and creative biblical expressions of art. To Bill, for always supporting the dreams of your wife and for being the best partner in life and in *Love-Wise*.

Jean E. Jones

To God, I extol you for drawing me up out of a pit, saving me, and remaking my life; you are amazing! To Clay, thank you for being the best husband ever, for reading every page of the manuscript, and for your insights and help. To Pam, thank you for believing in this project and pouring your talents and time into it; my friend—you amaze me! To Karla, for the gorgeous illustrations and creative eye. To Angie Wright, Kerrie Parlett, and Jean Strand for timing and proofing the lessons—you rock! To Hope, LaRae, Barb, Kathleen, and the rest at Harvest House for taking on this project and offering valuable insights. To Lori Marshall, Donna Jones, and Jeanne Whittaker for encouraging me to write these studies.

Karla Dornacher

Thank you, God, for being my eternal source of hope, and for allowing me to use my talents in this discovery book to glorify you and encourage others. Thank you, Jean and Pam, for inviting me to join you on this creative adventure into the depths of God's Word! Your talents truly amaze me! Thank you to the Harvest House team for being dedicated to strengthening the body of Christ with quality books that offer hope in Christ to a weary world. And thank you to my husband and best friend, Michael, for being the best encourager ever and for putting up with my creative craziness!

About the Authors

Pam Farrel

Pam Farrel is an international speaker, author of 45 books, including *7 Simple Skills for Every Woman* and the best-selling *Men Are Like Waffles, Women Are Like Spaghetti*. Pam has loved studying and teaching the Bible for over 40 years, and is wife to Bill Farrel. Together they enrich relationships through their ministry, *Love-Wise*. She and her husband enjoy the beach near their California home, often making family memories with their three sons, three daughters-in-law, and four grandchildren.

www.Love-Wise.com | Twitter: @pamfarrel | Facebook: billandpamfarrel and Creative Biblical Expressions

Jean E. Jones

Jean E. Jones loves teaching the Bible and writing Bible study guides that help people put God's words into actions. She's a contributing writer for *Crosswalk.com* and has written for *Today's Christian Woman* and *Home Life*. She speaks at women's events and conferences. She started teaching the Bible in high school and has served on women's ministry leadership teams for 20 years. Her husband, Dr. Clay Jones, is a professor in the Master of Arts in Christian Apologetics program at Biola University.

www.JeanEJones.net | Twitter: @JeanEstherJones | Facebook: jean.e.jones and Discovering Hope in the Psalms

Karla Dornacher

Karla Dornacher is an artist, best-selling author, and encourager. She has written and illustrated 16 books, including *Down a Garden Path* and *Love in Every Room*. Her art has been licensed for home decor and gift items, including fabric, flags, cards, calendars, and most recently, coloring books and Bible journaling bookmarks. Working in her home studio in the Pacific Northwest, where she lives with her husband and two cats, makes her heart happy. She finds her inspiration in her walk with God, the beauty of his creation, and time spent with family and friends.

www.karladornacher.com | Facebook: karladornacher

Blessed is the one who delights in the word of God

PSALM 1

As for me I have set MY KING on ZION my holy hill

Psalm 2:6

Create in ME a clean HEART O God

Psalm 51:10

the Lord is my shepherd

Psalm 23

GOD is the **STRENGTH** of my *heart* AND MY *portion* FOREVER

PSALM 73:26

WHY ARE YOU CAST DOWN *Oh my soul...* hope *in God* FOR I shall again... *praise* **Him** MY SALVATION AND MY GOD

PSALM 42:5-6a

I Will HOPE *continually*

PSALM 71:14

YOU HAVE TURNED FOR ME MY *mourning* into *dancing* AND *clothed* me with *gladness*

PSALM 30:11-12